BRITISH AIR POWER
IN THE 1980s
THE ROYAL AIR FORCE

AIR COMMODORE R.A.MASON
CBE, MA, RAF

GUILD PUBLISHING
LONDON

BRITISH AIR POWER
IN THE 1980s

THE ROYAL AIR FORCE

First published 1984

This edition published 1985
by Book Club Associates,
by arrangement with Ian Allan Ltd

Printed in the United Kingdom by
Ian Allan Printing Ltd

Previous page:
The TTTE: International co-operation in the air.
Crown copyright photo by Sgt. Brian Lawrence

This page:
**A Jaguar from No 41 Squadron displays its centre-line recce
pod.**

Contents

Acknowledgements

In compiling this update of the Royal Air Force's provision of air power to the nation's defence I have drawn upon generous advice, co-operation and assistance from many colleagues of all ranks throughout the Service. In particular I have benefited from the skills of many professional and amateur Service photographers whose work illustrates far more effectively than mere words could ever do the enormous extent and complexity of the tasks discharged every day, often under arduous conditions for very long hours in the air and on the ground, by the 93,000 men and women who proudly wear the light blue uniform. To them this book is dedicated, with respect and pride in their achievements.

I particularly wish to thank Miss Jean Bolton for her painstaking, tolerant and invariably good-humoured translation of frequently illegible manuscript; Mr Chris Hobson, the Head Librarian at the RAF Staff College Library, for his constant provision of source materials; and Air Cdre Phil Walker and all the PR staff throughout the Service without whose whole-hearted co-operation this book could not have been written.

Responsibility for factual accuracy, forecasts and opinion is entirely my own and in no way implies endorsement or otherwise by any department of the Ministry of Defence.

R. A. Mason

Foreword

by Air Chief Marshal Sir Keith Williamson GCB, AFC, ADC, Chief of the Air Staff

In this book Air Commodore Mason traces the evolution of British air power from its origins in the First World War, through the victories and sacrifices of the Second, right up to the present day – and in describing the many and varied roles of the Royal Air Force he focusses our attention on the contribution which air power makes both to Britain's deterrence posture and to the support of national interests around the world. The 1980s is proving to be an exciting period in our history, for the Royal Air Force is now in the middle of a major re-equipment programme which has been designed to sustain it in the forefront of the nation's defence well into the next century. So you will read of new aircraft and new weapons which are bringing about major developments and improvements right across our operational spectrum. But of course all this new technology still needs high quality people to operate it, and so the book also tells of the men and women who maintain the proud traditions of the Royal Air Force today and who prepare for and look forward to the challenges of the future – I am sure you will enjoy reading it.

Keith Williamson

1 The Evolution of British Air Power

Command of the Air

In 1893 Maj J. D. Fullerton of the Royal Engineers presented a paper at a meeting of military engineers in Chicago in which he prophesised that the impact of aeronautics foreshadowed 'as great a revolution in the art of war as the discovery of gunpowder', that future wars might well start with a great air battle, that 'the arrival of the aerial fleet over the enemy capital will probably conclude the campaign' and that 'command of the air' would be an essential prerequisite for all land and air warfare. Although Maj Fullerton does not seem to have included such prophetic statements in his addresses to British audiences during the next 20 years, his engineering friend, F. W. Lanchester, expressed in 1907 a similar view in the *Aeronautical Journal*:

'Under the conditions of the near future, the command of the air must become at least as essential to the safety of the empire as will be our continued supremacy of the high seas.'

In 1909 *Flight* became the official journal of the Aero Club, 'Devoted to the Interests, Practice and Progress of Aerial Locomotion and Transport'. On 15 May the editorial was titled 'Britain and the Command of the Air' and expressed concern at the nation's vulnerability to hostile aircraft even at their current stage of development, quite apart from the advent of 'all-weather aircraft'. That concern was swiftly reinforced when Bleriot crossed the Channel on 25 July in an aircraft of his own design. Britain could no longer rely on sea power alone for its defence.

Two years later Capt C. J. Burke wrote the first article on air power to be published by the journal of the Royal United Services Institute, first concentrating on the aeroplane as a reconnaissance vehicle, but then forcing home the lesson of Bleriot and the thinking of his civilian friends:

'May not the command of the air be as important to us in the future as the command of the sea is at the present moment?'

Below:
The day that geography was changed: Bleriot crosses the Channel on 25 July 1909 and command of the air becomes as important to Britain as command of the sea.

7

In 1913, Col Fullerton addressed the Royal United Services Institute on the theme of aeronautical progress and pursued his logic a stage further. After examining the concept of command of the air he concluded that:

'A separate organisation, with its own commander-in-chief, is essential for success and it is to be hoped that this will be realized before it is too late to take action in the matter.'

Not surprisingly, his view prompted stern disagreement from the major-general who was chairing the meeting and from several members present. The following year Lanchester, now a member of the Aeronautical Society and a regular contributor to the other journals, began his well-known series of articles in the magazine *Engineering*. He foresaw the employment of aircraft well behind the conventional battle lines, both on land and at sea, and stressed the further implications of offensive air power:

'It is safe to say that if during a battle it is found practicable to conduct air-raids and air attacks systematically over a considerable belt of territory in the rear of an enemy's lines, this belt will require to be defended.'

So, by 1914, five fundamental British ideas of air power had been formulated. First, that air power could contribute enormously to land and naval operations; second, that command of the air was as essential to Britain as was command of the sea; third, that to achieve command of the air an independent service needed to be established; fourth, that air power could reach out far beyond the lines of battle and strike at targets in the enemy's homelands; and, fifth, that by such offensive action one could force the enemy to divert essential resources to his own air defence.

From Balloon to Aeroplane
But as so often in the history of warfare, the period from the formulation of ideas to their successful application in battle was to be a long and arduous passage. Despite the pioneering work of men like Sir George Cayley, John Stringfellow, W. S. Henson and Percy Pilcher, British

Right:
The architect, the buildings and the men: Lord Trenchard inspecting apprentices at Halton in the 1920s.

Below:
A Handley Page V/1500 bomber of No 274 Squadron in 1919 at RAF Bircham Newton.

military air power originated not with the aeroplane but with the balloon. In 1878 a series of experiments with free and captive balloons was made at Woolwich Arsenal and a balloon equipment store was established. By the following year five balloons were in existence with a few trained officers and men drawn from the Royal Engineers. By 1884, when a balloon detachment was included in the RE units which accompanied an expedition to Bechuanaland, a factory, depot and school of instruction had been established at Chatham. Three balloon sections of the Royal Engineers served during the Boer War where they were used for directing artillery fire and reconnaissance. In 1905 the balloon factory moved to South Farnborough and there the Royal Aircraft Establishment had its origin. From that date on, balloon and aeroplane development, inspired by the activities of the Wright brothers, proceeded apace. On 1 April 1911 the Air Battalion of the Royal Engineers was formed. In 1912 the Battalion received the first British military aircraft – the Bleriot experimental aircraft No 1, which was accompanied by a certificate of airworthiness from the Army Aircraft Factory at South Farnborough, which read as follows:

BE 1 Certificate
This is to say that the aeroplane BE 1 has been thoroughly tested by me, and the mean speed over a ¾ mile course with a live load of 350lb and sufficient petrol for 1 hour's flight is 58–59mph. The rate of rising loaded as above has been tested up to 600ft and found to be at the rate of 155ft

Below:
Imperial Policing: a DH9A of No 8 Squadron over Baghdad, 1926.

per minute. The machine has been inverted and suspended from the centre and the wings loaded to three times the normal loading. On examination after this test the aeroplane showed no signs of defect.

(Signed) S HECKSTALL-SMITH
FOR SUPERINTENDENT ARMY AIRCRAFT
FACTORY 14 March 1912 SOUTH FARNBOROUGH

On 13 May 1912 the Royal Flying Corps was formed with a military wing, a naval wing, a Central Flying School, a Reserve, and the Royal Aircraft Factory at Farnborough. An Air Committee was established to co-ordinate the contribution of the two parent Services, but within a very short time the wings began to develop more in isolation than in harmony. The separation of the Royal Naval Air Service was officially recognised on 1 July 1914.

Air Power in World War 1
So, on the outbreak of war, there were in effect two British air forces. One, the Royal Flying Corps, was swiftly despatched to France with the primary mission to provide reconnaissance for the Army. The other remained located in Britain and in Belgium with a very new responsibility for the air defence of the United Kingdom and with somewhat imprecise ideas about its potential contribution to naval operations. The overall contribution of air power to Allied victory in World War 1 was comparatively limited. Major roles were largely in direct support of either the Army or the Navy. They included reconnaissance for either Army or Naval artillery and for troops and ship movements. From these roles evolved the natural inclination to stop the opposition doing the same thing which in turn led to air-to-air combat and the tactical manifestation

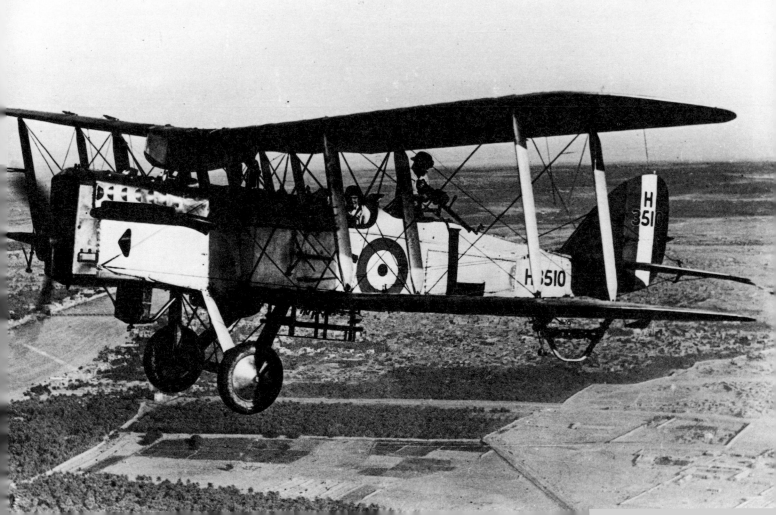

of command of the air: local air supremecy or superiority. As the war progressed and aircraft design became a little more sophisticated, air power began to reach out beyond the battle front to attack reserves, headquarters and communications centres on land, and submarine and other bases associated with the maritime war. The Royal Flying Corps became convinced of the importance of driving the enemy's aircraft from the skies over the battlefield, forcing him to devote more and more of his resources to air defence and thus giving valuable, if indirect, support to its own ground forces. Similarly, the RNAS discovered that the best way to reduce the enemy's submarine and airship threat to our own shipping was to destroy him in his own bases as well as hunting for him at sea.

But perhaps inevitably as the scale of the war increased, problems arose which could not be resolved by two infant and virtually separate air forces. There was wasteful competition for scarce resources, duplication of effort in some areas of activity and mutual neglect in others, and the perpetual friction between two autonomous agencies frantically seeking to meet the ever expanding demands of commanders for more aircraft, more crews, more technicians and more supporting equipment. A series of boards and committees was established in an attempt to resolve these problems but they were not invested with executive authority and were dependent on the goodwill of the individual service and civilian members. Consequently, co-operation and provision were constantly bedevilled by the personal rivalries and jealousies of senior commanders, politicians, press lords and industrialists. Problems of co-ordination were forced on to the attention of the general public by the lack of effective air defence against German bombing raids on London in 1917. Meanwhile there were already those who believed that air power should not be restricted by a subordinate role to the older Services but should reach out well beyond the battlefield to strike directly at the enemy's heartland and at his capacity to wage war; in other words, operations independent of either land or naval forces.

The Formation of the Royal Air Force
A Government committee headed by Field Marshal J. C. Smuts was appointed in 1917 to investigate the difficulties apparent in the waging of the war in the air. His report, presented to the Government on 17 August, has been called the Magna Carta of British air power. Smuts traced the previous attempts at co-ordination of Army and naval air services and stressed the inability of the existing Air Board to embark on a policy of its own. He then continued:

'The time is however rapidly approaching when that subordination of the Air Board and the Air Service can no longer be justified. Essentially, the position of an Air Service is quite different from that of the Artillery Arm ... (it) can be used as an independent means of war operations. Nobody who witnessed the attack on London on 7 July could have any doubt on that point. Unlike artillery, an air fleet can conduct extensive operations far from, and independently of, both Army and Navy. As far as at present can be foreseen, there is absolutely no limit to the scale of its future independent war use. And the day may not be far off when aerial operations with their devastation

of enemy lands and destruction of industrial and populace centres on a vast scale may become the principle operations of war, to which the older forms of military and naval operations may become secondary and subordinate.'

To realize the full potential of air power he recommended the creation of a separate air ministry, air staff and air service. He then concluded his report with a sentence almost identical to one used by Lanchester 10 years before:

'It is important for the winning of the war that we should not only secure air predominance, but secure it on a very large scale; and having secured it in this war we should make every effort and sacrifice to maintain it for the future. Air supremacy may in the long run become as important a factor in the defence of the Empire as sea supremacy.'

On 1 April 1918 the Royal Flying Corps and Royal Naval Air Service were amalgamated to form the Royal Air Force.

Jonah's Gourd
In the exhausted postwar years, not everyone was convinced of the need to retain an independent Royal Air Force. It was argued that it would be less costly to run if returned to its constituent naval and army parts. Some admirals and generals believed that air power could best be applied in the national interest if projected simply as an extension of land and sea power. Other idealistic individuals failed to recognise that the democratisation of war had, perhaps permanently, blurred the dividing line between the combatant who carried the weapon and the civilian who made it. Such individuals opposed the new service on the mistaken grounds that it existed only to wage war on the unprotected and innocent. Overall, the very existence of the Royal Air Force hung in the balance until the Salisbury Committee Report of 1923 finally gave government sanction to its independence.

Fortunately for both the country and the RAF, the wisdom and vision of two powerful men, Winston Churchill, Minister for War and Air in 1919, and his Chief of the Air Staff, Air Marshal Trenchard, succeeded in persuading the government to acknowledge the need for the Third Service.

'It seems to me' wrote Sir Hugh Trenchard on 11 September 1919, 'that there are two alternatives:

1 To use the air simply as a means of conveyance, captained by chauffeurs, weighted by the Navy and Army personnel, to carry out reconnaissance for the Navy or Army, drop bombs at places specified by them immediately affecting local operations or observe for their artillery.
2 To really make an air service which will encourage and develop airmanship, or better still, the air spirit, like the naval spirit, and to make it a force that will profoundly alter the strategy of the future ...'

The blueprint for the second alternative was set out in a Government White Paper, 'Permanent Organization of the Royal Air Force', published in December 1919. Known familiarly as 'The Trenchard Memorandum' it started by

Above:
The legend: R. J. Mitchell's Supermarine Spitfire.

Left:
The Supermarine S6B, Schneider Trophy winner in 1931 and progenitor of the Spitfire, being prepared for the decisive race.

summarising the contemporary condition of the Royal Air Force which:

'... could in fact, be compared to the prophet Jonah's gourd. The necessities of war created it in a night, but the economies of peace had to a large extent caused it to wither in a day, and the necessity had to be faced of replacing it with a plant of deeper root.'

That deeper root was to be achieved by concentrating on:

'... providing for the needs of the moment as far as they can be foreseen and on laying the foundations of a highly trained and efficient force which, though not capable of expansion in its present form, can be made so without any drastic alteration should necessity arise in years to come. Broadly speaking, the principle has been to reduce service squadrons to the minimum considered essential for our garrisons overseas with a very small number in the United Kingdom as a reserve, and to concentrate the whole of the remainder of our resources on perfecting the training of officers and men.'

The Royal Air Force College at Cranwell, the Apprentice Training School at Halton, the Staff College at Andover, the Auxiliary Air Force and ultimately the Royal Air Force Volunteer Reserve all owed their origins to this remarkable document.

Consolidation between the Wars

Two years later, further impetus was given to the Service when a conference was held at Cairo in 1921 to determine the most effective way of administering several territories held by Britain under mandate from the League of Nations. Proposals by Churchill and Trenchard to allocate the major responsibility for policing of the territories to the Royal Air Force were accepted. Subsequently RAF aircraft carried out peacekeeping operations in Iraq, Kurdistan, Aden and the North West Frontier at a fraction of the cost and in much less time than would have been required for large garrisons of troops.

Nor were activities overseas restricted to peacekeeping. Flt Lts Alcock and Brown had already fired the nation's imagination by their record-breaking non-stop flight across the Atlantic in 1919. In the following decade many more flights were made across the globe, pioneering the imperial air routes – to Cape Town, to Singapore and to Australia.

At home, the public's interest was captured by the annual RAF displays at Hendon and by frequent attempts by serving officers on either speed, altitude or long distance records. In 1937 the world altitude record was raised incredibly to 53,937ft by Flt Lt M. J. Adam in an all-wooden Bristol 138. But perhaps most famous were the victories of RAF pilots in the races for the Schneider Maritime Trophy, won outright for Britain in 1931 by Flt Lt J. N. Boothman in the Rolls-Royce engined Supermarine S6B, precursor of the Spitfire, the RAF's most famous fighter.

The Shadows of War
In 1933 the Geneva disarmament conference collapsed; in the same year Hitler came to power in Germany. The need to increase the 74 squadrons of the Royal Air Force was obvious and from 1934 onwards further squadrons were added each year in an increasingly strenuous attempt to keep pace with the even more rapidly expanding Luftwaffe.

There was, however, much to do. Not only had a new generation of aeroplanes to be built – the Blenheims, Wellingtons and Whitleys – but the air and ground crews had to be recruited and trained to fly and to service them. Longer ranges and better aircraft performance demanded improved navigational equipment; location of targets in European weather in the face of well trained opposition would require additional skills to those learned flying against relatively undefended targets under the Middle Eastern sun, no matter how valuable that experience had been in other ways. The impact of years of financial stringency could not be eradicated in a few months.

In 1939 the Air Staff wanted more time, to re-equip the fighter squadrons with the Hurricane and Spitfire, to perfect new navigation and bombing techniques and to complete the chain of radar stations under construction round the south and east coasts of these islands. It was not to be granted all the time it required, but the breathing space between the invasion of Poland and the drive to Dunkirk was to prove just sufficient.

Air Power comes of Age
From 1939 to 1945 the RAF served in every theatre of war. In 1940 von Runstedt's armies outflanked the Maginot Line, overran the few British airfields in France and paved the way for Operation 'Sea Lion'. But Adm Doenitz would not countenance a sea-borne invasion until British air power had been eliminated. While Bomber Command attacked the invasion barges in their harbours, Fighter Command fought off the Luftwaffe's attempt to establish command of the air over southern England.

The details of that battle are well known. Names such as Dowding, Deere, Bader and Lacey became legend; many others are remembered silently and locally in Britain, the Commonwealth, France, Poland and Czechoslovakia. By the end of October the threat of invasion had passed and slowly the air war was taken back to the enemy.

As the next generation of bombers – the Stirlings, Halifaxes and Lancasters – began to enter service, Bomber Command, under its new Commander-in-Chief Sir Arthur Harris, planned to undermine Germany's ability to continue the war by destroying both its industrial heart and its will to fight. Progress was slow and costly; bombers were needed in the Middle East and for Coastal Command's anti U-boat war. German fighter pilots were as skilful and courageous in defending their homeland as their British counterparts had been in 1940; German scientists had developed their own effective radar screen. But the drain on the German war effort was enormous. In 1943 more shells were produced for German anti-aircraft guns than for their anti-tank guns on the entire Eastern front. Moreover, in the darker days of the war, before the Anglo-American alliance had gathered strength, while the Soviet Union was fighting for its very existence and when British victories on land were few and far between, the British public could find reassurance in the sound of Rolls-Royce engines at dusk and dawn and the news of exploits of men

like Gibson, Cheshire and Nettleton. Bomber Command lost nearly 60,000 aircrew, but while strategists may still debate their contribution, Albert Speer had no doubt. He asserted that the loss of the air war over Germany was his country's most critical defeat.

Meanwhile, aircraft of Coastal Command, working closely with the Royal Navy, slowly closed the Atlantic to the U-boat. Their task was often lonely and unglamorous, but in 1943 they broke the tightening German blockade, enabling the convoys to get through with their American equipment and forces. Without that freedom of the sea, the invasion of Europe Operation 'Overlord', could not have been contemplated.

The last year of the war saw the RAF and the USAAC, drawing upon the experience gained by the Desert Air Force under Air Marshal Tedder, ranging over Western Europe in support of Gen Eisenhower's armies. The Normandy battlefields were isolated, German reinforcements interdicted and, with the exception of its last desperate offensive on New Year's Day 1945, the Luftwaffe was obliterated as a fighting force. Allied troops rested, regrouped, resupplied, reinforced and attacked with little or no thought for air defence. Experiences on those same French and Belgium roads five years previously were forgotten beneath the security of allied command of the air.

Finally, across the other side of the globe, air power made its most dramatic and final contribution. The ashes of Hiroshima and Nagasaki were the culmination of the dreams and nightmares of those who had foreseen the ultimate impact of strategic air power, even if their vision could never have foreseen that such devastation could be the product of just two bombs. Although these two weapons were built and dropped by Britain's ally, their direct and indirect influence on the future direction of the Royal Air Force and British air power would be all-pervasive.

British Air Power in the Nuclear Age
History has already shown us that the seeds of the Cold War had been sown before the defeat of Germany. Since 1945 the RAF's major role in the defence of the UK has been its contribution to a common deterrent posture of the Western allies against the Soviet Union. For the greater part of the period, Bomber Command provided the nation's strategic nuclear deterrent force. Planned in the aftermath of the German war, first the Valiants, then the Victors and Vulcans, entered service in the 1950s. Later equipped with the Blue Steel stand-off bomb, the V-Force ably discharged its responsibility until relieved by the Royal Navy's Polaris ballistic missile submarines in 1969.

Fighter defence of the UK was provided first by Meteors and Venoms, then by Javelins and Hunters, until the Defence White Paper of 1957, in considering that the threat to this country would in future originate mainly from missiles rather than manned bombers, heralded a drastic reduction in the strength of Fighter Command. Subsequent developments in Soviet manned aircraft have in retrospect made that judgement, to say the least, premature.

In addition to strategic defence and nuclear deterrence, the RAF made major contributions to all three postwar major Western – orientated alliances: NATO, CENTO and SEATO, until national economic stringencies once again forced reduction in defence expenditure. This time however, unlike the period after 1919, the reductions were accompanied by withdrawals from overseas alliance commitments. Thus squadrons were progressively withdrawn from Singapore, Bahrein, Aden and Cyprus to concentrate our major defence effort in Europe.

Yet, although officially at peace, and despite withdrawals, the Royal Air Force has actually mounted operations of one sort or another, in many different countries, in every year since 1945. From 1948 to 1949, in co-operation with the USAF and French Air Force, the Berlin airlift denied that city to the Soviet Union. RAF flying boat squadrons, as well as other elements of air and ground crews, supported the UN Expeditionary Force in Korea. From 1948 to 1960, operations were flown against terrorists in Malaya: ground forces were rapidly deployed and supplied; casualties were evacuated; surveillance patrols mounted and direct offensive support delivered. In Cyprus and Kenya similar support was provided in the fight against the EOKA and Mau Mau terrorists. In the Radfan, air-to-ground attacks contributed to the security of the Aden Protectorate prior to our withdrawal. At Suez in 1956 the efficiency of the RAF operations should be clearly separated in memory from the aftermath of the political debacle.

Left:
An earlier generation of RAF Regiment armoured cars at Gutersloh in 1947.

Right:
A Vulcan in its primary, original role, carrying the Blue Steel stand-off nuclear weapon in 1967.

On some occasions the mere presence of the Royal Air Force has had a restraining effect on vociferous would-be opponents – in Kuwait in 1960, in the Indonesian confrontation in 1965 and more recently on two occasions in the territory of Belize. At other times, for instance during the Cyprus emergency in 1974, the swift and timely arrival of RAF combat aircraft has served as a sharp reminder of the strategic flexibility of air power.

As in the prewar period, the reputation of the Service has also been sustained by more peaceful operations. Victims of natural disasters in Turkey, Nigeria, Kenya, Somalia, Nepal and many other regions have benefited from the ability of RAF pilots to land emergency supplies on hastily prepared air strips under the most difficult conditions. At home, RAF search and rescue helicopters have saved countless lives at sea and helped in the rescue of many others from remote areas on land. Consecutive generations of aerobatic teams – such as the Black Arrows, Blue Diamonds and Red Arrows – have demonstrated their skills, not just at one airfield as at Hendon before the war, but all over the world. Speed and long range records have been set over the North Pole, to South Africa, Australia and New Zealand, and perhaps most spectacularly by a Harrier of No 1 Squadron in the London to New York air race of 1969.

The Falklands Campaign

Unexpectedly, the RAF found itself at war again in the South Atlantic in 1982, in truly combined operations with Army and Royal Navy colleagues. Air power was seen to be neither independent nor subordinate but, as any impartial observer should have seen half a century ago, complementary to land and sea power. The Fleet denied surface reinforcement to the Argentine, drove off the Argentinian navy, convoyed and protected land forces despatched to liberate the islands, and shared the air defence and ground attack tasks with RAF Harriers. The ground forces endured the fighting on the islands and forced a numerically superior enemy to yield. In addition to training the RNAS Harrier pilots and providing some of the Sea Harrier crews, the RAF complemented the sister services in a number of ways. Initially, Nimrods of No 42 Squadron flew anti-submarine patrols ahead of the Task Force as it moved south, and maintained contact with the friendly nuclear submarines deployed ahead of the group. Later, Nimrod Mk 2 reinforcements flew reconnaissance missions between the islands and the Argentinian mainland to give early warning of any attempt to interfere with Task Force operations. As the Nimrods were progressively equipped for air-to-air refuelling, and carried a variety of anti-surface weapons and Sidewinder air-to-air missiles, so the sorties became longer and more offensive, although in the event no Nimrod pilot had an opportunity to claim a fighter role for his four-engined maid of all work. Almost 50% of the RAF's transport force was committed to the operation: by 16 June for example the movements staff at Wideawake Airfield on Ascension Island had handled 13,970,000lb of freight. As the Air Commander of the operation, Air Marshal Sir John Curtiss, subsequently observed: 'This operation must rank with the Berlin Airlift in achievement.' The Hercules also was fitted rapidly with an in-flight refuelling probe and dropped urgent spares and other supplies to the Task Force as it lay off the Falklands. On 1 May a further dimension was added to

the South Atlantic confrontation when a Vulcan of No 50 Squadron, deployed from RAF Waddington, attacked the runway at Port Stanley. The stick of 21 bombs straddled the airfield, leaving one crater in the centre of the runway. The attack however had far more significance than the damage caused at the time. The Vulcan, with considerable Victor tanker support, had flown a round attack trip of 8,500 miles, the longest bombing raid in aviation history. That combat radius put the majority of Argentinian mainland airfields well within range. Doubtless any such attack would have had political repercussions, and would have required extensive resource allocation. But the extended Vulcan threat could not be ignored by Argentinian air defences and perhaps when Argentinian operational records ultimately become available, the real extent of the threat and the diversion of AAF resources which it prompted may become apparent. In addition of course, the vulnerability of the Stanley airfield was underlined. It was clearly no place for forward deployment of Super Etendards or Mirages, even had the AAF had the inclination to take such a tactically valuable step. The Vulcan attacks on airfield and associated radars were

14

supplemented by day by the Harrier GR3s of No 1 Squadron and the Sea Harriers, as part of the overall close air support, interdiction, reconnaissance and PR contribution of the VSTOL aircraft. While the air attacks did not prevent the AAF flying C-130 supply and evacuation sorties by night, they did deny the airfield to any jet combat aircraft, for which the Task Force had good reason to be thankful.

Tactical airlift was tragically curtailed by the loss of the container ship *Atlantic Conveyor* together with three of the four Chinook helicopters despatched to the theatre and all the Chinook spares. The sole survivor from No 18 Squadron flew continuously throughout the battle, making maximum use of its heavy lift capability, becoming known to the troops as the Flying Angel, no doubt in part because of the alternative it offered to 'Yomping' through the islands' peat bogs and mud.

It was however the unsung activities of the air to air refuelling Victor squadrons which underpinned much of air power's contribution to the campaign. They refuelled Vulcans, Harriers, Hercules, Nimrods and each other to maintain combat operations and transit over distances akin to those between the United Kingdom and India. In the early stages they also flew maritime reconnaissance sorties in support of the highly secret advance force led by HMS *Antrim* to repossess South Georgia. Six months after the end of hostilities, Sir John Curtiss wrote:

'Air power is a vital and flexible adjunct to any military operation. No single Service is independent of the others and jointery must not only be preached, it must also be practised. Everything we have claimed for AAR as a force multiplier and force enabler has been confirmed by this operation and I believe that all front line aircraft should be AAR capable. I also believe if the shopping list were mine – that any aircraft operated in the combat zone should be adequately equipped for self defence.'

British air power had come a long way since Lt-Col J. T. C. Moore-Brabazon MC, MP had made the first British free-flight in the British Isles at Shellbeach on the Isle of Sheppey in May 1909. Yet the dramatic contribution to the campaign in the South Atlantic was but one, albeit powerful, example of the long range, rapid response, precision, strength and flexibility of modern air power. These qualities can confer considerable support to the statesman in peacetime, and should deterrence fail, to the commander in combat, as a survey of the role of British air power in support of foreign and defence interests fully illustrates.

2 The Roles of British Air Power in the 1980s

For many generations it was important for Britons to remember that 75% of the earth's surface was covered by sea. The 22 miles separating Dover from Calais undoubtedly had a major influence on the relative independence which Britain was able to enjoy from mainland Europe for several thousand years. However, since Bleriot flew the Channel in 1909 it has been necessary to recall on several occasions that all the earth is covered by air. The modern Royal Air Force exists to apply air power in the nation's defence and in support of more far-reaching foreign policy interests. In practice, air power cannot be easily separated from sea power and land power. As the Falklands campaign most recently and clearly illustrated, the three are required to be complementary to each other in wartime.

What is Modern Air Power?

On occasion in the past the nature of air power itself and one or two of its specialised functions have become confused. In the immediate aftermath of World War 2 air power was synonymous with strategic bombardment, as it had frequently been in the minds of the early air power theorists. In the mid-1980s however, it is clearly far more than that. It may be defined practically as 'The ability to project military force by or from a platform in the third dimension, above the surface of the earth.' The ability to project air power may be likened to the old naval concept of a fleet in being: a formidable force just over the horizon or even in home port, which by its very existence was a potential force which could be called upon by the government of the time. Today, a wing of Tornados in Germany may be similarly regarded. It may not actually be applying military force but it displays a formidable ability to do so. Ability may be translated into the actual application of air power either directly by bombing, by missile delivery, by interception; or indirectly: by the provision of reconnaissance, by air mobility, by supply dropping or even by the provision of aid to a civil authority. Air power can be applied by both armies and navies in addition to their primary roles: the specialist forces of the Army Air Corps and the Royal Naval Air Service are highly professional exponents. But the 'third dimension' is the specialist domain of the Royal Air Force in exactly the same way that the sea is the primary element of the Royal Navy and the ground that of the Army. Moreover, air power differs markedly from sea and land power in that it possesses certain characteristics in proportions markedly different from those possessed by either of the other two.

Below:
A Chipmunk looking over the Berlin Wall.

The first is speed. The highly trained armoured divisions of World War 2 could cover 100 miles a day. We have recently seen a rapidly assembled naval task force sail 300 miles in a day. A VC10 or a Phantom on the other hand covers eight miles in a minute. The practical implications of those comparisons were seen in the South Atlantic war. The Shackleton Report of July 1976 had recommended that the runway at Port Stanley airport should be extended at a cost of £3.5–4 million, to take longer range, heavier aircraft. The Government of the day decided not to act upon that particular recommendation. Thereby, British air power was denied an opportunity to forestall the Argentinian invasion. The ability of long-range, land based air power to deter or to pre-empt such activity within a possibly short warning time, to reassure friends and quite simply to raise the apparent cost of any military adventure by a political opponent was thus lost. Strategic, high speed response at long range is the prerogative of air power, whether used independently as in the mere presence of a detachment of Phantoms, Jaguars or Nimrods, or when co-ordinated with land or sea power. Like any other kind of military power, air power cannot on its own gain a political objective, least of all for a democracy. But it can produce more favourable circumstances for the diplomat to exploit. Because such an opportunity was not taken in the Falklands before 1982, military power to restore such circumstances had to be called upon at infinitely greater expense and risk. Meanwhile, long after the maritime exclusion zones around the island had been defined by the British Government before real hostilities broke out, the Argentinian Air Force continued to fly in large numbers of men and equipment. In the event, the time taken by the British Task Force to sail 7,000 miles gave the UK time to mobilise diplomatic support, but at the cost of a heavily reinforced opponent. By contrast, the advantage of having access to a well-equipped strategic airfield was apparent in 1983 when at the height of the Lebanese crisis a detachment of Buccaneers reached Cyprus within 24 hours to reinforce British diplomacy and support the peacekeeping forces.

The second important characteristic of air power is its relative combat radius or reach. A battery of artillery for example can engage targets up to 20 miles distance. Surface ships can engage 25 miles over the horizon and up to 250 miles by using ship-borne Sea Harriers. Nimrod, on

Left:
An attack with retarded 1,000lb bombs by Tornado GR1s of No 9 Squadron illustrates the speed and firepower that are such important characteristics of air power. *BAe*

Below:
Tankers and transports – long range air power deployed at Ascension. *Author*

the other hand, threatens targets within a combat radius of 2,000 miles while Tornado with in-flight refuelling could attack targets deep in Eastern Europe from bases in the west of England. Added to both speed and reach is the ability to concentrate very heavy firepower in both time and space. One may compare the six-gun Abbot battery and its firing of 30 rounds to deliver 1,000lb of high explosive over several minutes with the 16,000lb bomb load of one Tornado effective in a few seconds of impact.

The fourth characteristic is the potential which air power has for mounting different kinds of operation from the one weapons platform. Sometimes this flexibility has been the product of pragmatic innovation in response to unusual circumstances, as was the case in Nimrod and Victor employment in the South Atlantic. Increasingly it is planned from the outset of aircraft design, as exemplified by the Tornado, designed for use against airfields, communications, armour, surface shipping and other aircraft as well as for reconnaissance.

Clearly, these characteristics are all possessed in some degree or other by naval and land forces and in any decision as to their complementary use, the question of comparative costs and desired objectives must be borne in mind. Nevertheless, the combined characteristics of high

Above:
A gentle showing of the flag: a detachment of No 12 Squadron Buccaneers at Gibraltar.

Below:
A Gazelle of No 12 Flight, Army Air Corps simulates the search for post raid bomb damage in an exercise at RAF Wildenrath.

18

speed, long reach, heavy fire power and flexibility in operation are unique to air power.

The Contribution of British Air Power to NATO Strategy

After 40 years of comparative peace in Europe, despite the presence on both sides of the Iron Curtain of more destructive fire power than at any time in European history, the significance of air power in NATO strategic planning is still increasing. Indeed, as ways continue to be sought to reduce the reliance of the Western alliance on nuclear weapons, conventional war fighting capability will become even more important. It is no coincidence that the Soviet Union has for many years paid considerable attention to the lessons learned about air power from World War 2. It had been the spearhead of the German Blitzkreig; in Figher Command it had prevented the invasion of the United Kingdom; in Coastal Command it had shared equally with sea power in the defeat of the U-boat; it had first isolated British forces in North Africa by destroying naval reinforcements along the Mediterranean and then it severed Rommel's own supply routes. It had

sustained clandestine operations in many theatres; it had provided additional mobility and reinforcements over long distances; it had ravaged German industry to such an extent that the bulk of Hitler's aircraft industry was driven to produce fighters to protect itself; it had crippled the Italian Navy; smashed the United States' traditional sea power at Pearl Harbor and then in turn decided the war in the Pacific. Ultimately, it delivered the bombs on Hiroshima and Nagasaki. Every commander on land and sea had to include air power as a dominant factor in his planning. Command of the air was a prerequisite for success in every kind of military operation.

In 1985, the potential role of air power in peace and war is perhaps even more pervasive. The strategy of the North Atlantic Treaty Organisation is familiarly summarized as 'flexibility in response' which as the NATO Handbook explains:

'Places increased emphasis on conventional defences. Since the Soviet Union has reached a position of approximate parity with the United States in the field of strategic

Air Power and the Alliance

The effectiveness of British air power was seen during the Falkland Islands campaign. However, the Royal Air Force would have a primary role to play as part of NATO's air power in any conflict with the Warsaw Pact.

Left:
No 230 Squadron and friends at Gutersloh, with a Luftwaffe UH-1D in the foreground.
Crown copyright photo by SAC Pete Boardman

Below:
A RAF Puma of No 230 Squadron and Belgian soldiers in the NATO exercise 'Summer Tiger' 1982.
Crown copyright photo by SAC Pete Boardman

nuclear weapons, NATO cannot rely on the possession of such weapons alone to deter major conventional attacks. They must be associated with strong conventional forces as integral elements of the overall NATO deterrent.'

British Defence Forward Policy Statements have identified the four main roles in which the armed forces contribute to the collective deterrent: the provision of independent strategic and theatre nuclear forces committed to the Alliance; the direct defence of the United Kingdom homeland; a major land and air contribution on the European mainland; and the deployment of a major maritime capability in the Eastern Atlantic and the Channel. British air power contributes to the theatre nuclear forces; it is the mainstay of the direct defence of the United Kingdom homeland; it is a major contributor to the European mainland commitment; and a major partner in the maritime capability in the Eastern Atlantic and the Channel.

Top:
NATO Boeing E-3A Sentry from Geilenkirchen visiting RAF Wildenrath. This remarkable AWACS aircraft can provide comprehensive surveillance to a range of at least 230 miles and has an unrefuelled endurance of more than 11 hours.

Above:
A USAF F-15 Eagle and CAF CF-104 Starfighter at the NATO 'Tiger Meet' 1982.
Crown copyright photo by Cpl Geoff Card

But for the Alliance to implement the strategy of flexibility in response, three major problems must be overcome. First, NATO in-position forces are out-numbered in Europe in soldiers, tanks, artillery and aircraft. Second, in all foreseeable circumstances the opponent would have the advantage of choosing the time, the place and method of his attack and we know that his strategic doctrine emphasises surprise, speed and concentration of force in the offensive. Therefore the third problem is that reinforcement of any region in NATO from another must overcome obvious geographical obstacles – the Atlantic, the North Sea, the Baltic, the Mediterranean and the many mountainous regions between them. Consequently, the Alliance has come to rely heavily on air power to redress local numerical inferiority and to provide rapid reinforcement and resupply. Thus, in the first hours of any European conflict, the demands on NATO's air forces would be heavy. The RAF could be expected to be committed in many areas. Our Harriers, Jaguars and Tornados would provide offensive firepower in support of our ground forces; they would seek to disrupt, dislocate and destroy enemy second-echelon armed forces essential to maintain the Warsaw Pact momentum. Jaguars and Tornados would dislocate the Warsaw Pact air activities by attacks on airfields. Phantoms, and in due course the projected multinational combat aircraft, would provide local air superiority above NATO's ground forces while reconnaissance Tornados and Jaguars would contribute to the provision of intelligence to ground commanders in a confused and fluid combat. Meanwhile, Buccaneers, Nimrods and Phantoms would be working with other Allied units over the Eastern Atlantic, the Norwegian Sea and the North Sea providing support to maritime forces against air, surface and submarine attack. The pivotal position of the British Isles as the forward deployment area for Allied forces from North America and the rear support area for the European Theatre would be defended by Phantoms and Tornado F2s working with the Tristar, Victor and VC10 tankers, co-ordinated by the Nimrod AWACS aircraft and reinforced by day-fighter short range Hawks. Throughout the Alliance area Hercules, VC10s, those Tristars not being used for in-flight refuelling, Pumas and Chinooks would add a strategic and tactical mobility to our ground forces. If required, a proportion of the Jaguars and Tornados could also contribute to SACEUR's theatre nuclear response.

Since the formulation of NATO's strategy in the late 1960s, the strength of the Warsaw Pact has increased enormously. In 1981 the Soviet Union is believed to have spent 20% of its defence budget on research and development. Of that, two-fifths was allocated to the air forces. In the same year it spent 45% of all its defence budget on various aspects of air power. Half as much again was spent on new aircraft as on ships, armour and fighting vehicles put together. The implications of that expenditure at that time are formidable. The procurement process for aircraft – that is the various steps from the formulation of the concept, through selection of the design, production, test flying and ultimately entry into squadron service – can take anything from five to 15 years. For example, some prototype aircraft seen at Moscow in 1967 were still entering Soviet squadrons 15 years later. It is therefore possible to form a reasonably confident estimate about the likely size, shape and potential of the Soviet air forces in the later 1980s and through into the 1990s.

Since 1960 the Soviet Union has steadily increased the quality and numbers of surface-to-air defences deployed across Eastern Europe and throughout the Soviet Union. An interlaced system comprising radar-guided rapid

firing guns like the ZSU-23/4, short range radar-guided and heat-seeking missiles such as SAMs 10, 11 and 12, and high altitude SAM 5s, has allowed Soviet aircraft production to concentrate more and more on multi-role and offensive aircraft rather than the traditional fighter. For example, the 'Flogger' fighter which entered service in the early 1970s now flies in several configurations equipped for ground attack operations. Nevertheless the Soviet air forces are continuing to deploy increasingly sophisticated fighters. The two-seat MiG-31 'Foxhound' is a development of the record breaking MiG-25, apparently designed as a supersonic high altitude interceptor with improved radar and weapon-carrying capability. It is likely to operate with the Soviets' own AWACS aircraft, the Il-76 modification, 'Mainstay-A'. Another new Mikoyan design, MiG-29 'Fulcrum', seems to be a dual-role fighter which could ultimately replace the MiG-23, the MiG-21 and the Sukhoi 'Fitter' range of aircraft. A third new tactical combat aircraft under development is the Su-27 'Flanker' which has been provisionally assessed as a pure air superiority fighter possibly in the F-15 and F-14 range. Soviet offensive air power has been considerably strengthened by deployment of a large and rapidly increasing helicopter force of Mi-8 'Hip' and Mi-24 'Hind' helicopters which are used as gunships ahead of and together with armoured formations, as troop carriers and possibly even as anti-helicopter fighters. This short range attacking force in turn has released medium range aircraft such as 'Fencer' and the new Su-25 'Frogfoot', similar in configuration and apparently in operational concept to the USAF A-10, to adopt more free ranging and longer operations. The older long range bombers and maritime attack aircraft have been supplemented by 'Backfire' and will probably be supplemented further by the new 'Blackjack' strategic bomber. This latter aircraft is apparently much larger than the American B-1B and could be designed to carry newly developed Soviet air-launched cruise missiles. Moreover, the Soviet equivalent of Bomber Command has been reorganised to give greater flexibility and deployment between possible theatres. Meanwhile the transport force is being expanded even further with the development of a large wide-bodied military transport given the NATO reporting name of 'Condor'. Even without 'Condor', the range and payload of the Russian transport force has been trebled over the last 15 years. Overall, the ability of the Warsaw Pact to interdict NATO reinforcements and attack NATO airfields, command and control centres, and nuclear sites, as well as to provide heavy close offensive air support to its own land forces, has been considerably increased. Meanwhile the essential tasks of the NATO air forces of offensive support and deep aerial penetration have been complicated by the widespread strengthening of Warsaw Pact air defences.

It is no exaggeration to state that while any struggle for Europe would be likely to be decided on land, victory would go to the alliance which had been able to make its air power do what was expected of it. Fortunately NATO strategy is based on deterrence. British air power would only be employed if that deterrence policy had failed. It rests on a triad of strategic nuclear, theatre nuclear and conventional forces. If the Soviet Union should ever conclude that a political objective in Europe could be pursued by force, such a conclusion might well follow an appreciation that success could be achieved before Western agreement to use nuclear weapons. In that case, the highest premium would be placed by the Warsaw Pact on speed and concentration of force to present the West with a fait accompli following either a conventional, chemical or a limited nuclear attack or indeed any combination of the three. For such a venture, Soviet estimation of the possibilities of success would clearly be an assessment of the ability of Western air power to destroy, or simply to delay and disrupt the operation to such an extent that the risk of nuclear retaliation, before local success had been achieved, would be unacceptable. The fundamental contribution of Alliance air power, in which Britain plays such an essential part, is therefore in peacetime to strengthen the traditional, conventional concept of deterrence – quite simply to induce in an opponent the doubt that he will be able to achieve his objective without unacceptable costs. The more effective NATO air power is seen to be in peacetime, the less likely it is ever to be called upon to operate in war.

Beyond NATO

Fortunately, the contribution of British air power to deterrence and to NATO war strategies is, and hopefully will remain, a subject simply for speculation. But further afield, in the third world, air power is increasingly being applied by many nations. The presence or availability of military force has long been an important diplomatic instrument. A traditional role of sea power has been to demonstrate the interest, influence or patronage of a state

Right:
Luftwaffe Phantom F-4F on visit to Gutersloh.
Crown copyright photo by SAC Pete Boardman

Below:
A Danish Air Force F-16B visiting RAFG. The F-16 has replaced F-104s in service in the NATO countries of Belgium, Denmark, the Netherlands and Norway, in addition to service with the USAF and several non-NATO nations.

to distant regions. Indeed Adm Ghorshkov has widely publicised that very objective for the contemporary Soviet Navy. Now, increasingly, air power is being used in a similar manner. A recent government Defence Policy Statement underlined the importance of the need for the United Kingdom, and indeed the Alliance as a whole, to take account of the threat to Western security interests outside the NATO area. It observed:

'Although our capability to carry out operations in the rest of the world is necessarily not comparable with that intended to discharge our NATO roles, in either scale or nature, it can still exert an influence out of all proportion to the resources involved.'

The presence of a detachment of Harriers in Belize is a signal to Guatemala that any action against its neighbour will need to take into account the British interest. Similarly the deployment of a handful of Jaguars or a couple of Nimrods to the Gulf area would not, in itself, remove any threat to the area or resolve the problems in it, but they would be a token of British commitment, a reassurance to

SBA Support For British Forces Lebanon

Above:

The British Forces in Lebanon, 110 strong, received all their logistic support, medical back-up and operational RAF support from the British Sovereign Bases in Cyprus. The picture includes the main elements of this support:

1 – A *Chinook helicopter of No 7 Squadron* RAF detachment transported the resupply of men and material needs when Beirut International Airport was closed to Hercules transports.

2 – The six *Buccaneers of No 12 and 208 Squadrons* were deployed to Cyprus on 9 September 1983 to provide air support, should the need have arisen, to protect the British contingent with the MNF in Beirut.

3 – The *Phantom Mk 2s* provided the Buccaneers with their own integral combat air patrol support should the Buccaneers have had to deploy over the Lebanon.

4 – The *Army and Royal Air Force medical services* based in Cyprus were available to provide medevac and treatment facilities.

5 – The *Ferret Scout Car Mk 2s* were the patrol vehicles of the British Forces Lebanon. In the event of repairs being required, if beyond the capabilities of British Forces Lebanon, the vehicles were flown back to *48 Command Workshops,*

Royal Electrical and Mechanical Engineers, at RAF Akrotiri, repaired and flown back to Beirut.

6 – The *Wessex Mk 2s of No 84 Squadron RAF* were used frequently for the passage of VIP's, visitors, men and equipment to and from Beirut. They were also available to provide medical evacuation if necessary.

7 – The officers and men of *No 23 Postal and Courier Service, Royal Engineers* ensured that official and private mail reached the soldier on the ground.

8 – The *Royal Signals in Cyprus* were responsible for communications between Cyprus and Beirut and for the repair and maintenance of the communications equipment in Beirut.

9 – The officers and men of the *Royal Army Ordnance Corps Supply Depots* in Cyprus provided all the vehicles stores, rations and other items required in Beirut.

10 – The *ammunition technicians of the RAOC* provided the necessary ammunition advice and bomb disposal assistance to British Forces Lebanon.

11 – The Royal Engineers of *62 (Cyprus) Support Squadron Royal Engineers* carried out an extensive number of engineering tasks in Beirut.

12 – *No 10 Port Squadron Royal Corps of Transport* gave assistance by transporting men and material to Beirut in the Range Target and Towing Launch *Michael Murphy VC,* and in their Ramp Powered Lighters.

Technology and Air Power

The importance of technology for the employment of modern air power is always evident – airframes, engines, avionics and weapons are all products of an advanced industrial system. These pictures represent some of the less often seen elements of technology and air power.

Left:
Man is not lost – in the South Atlantic, with Hercules navigator Flt Lt Steve Andrews supplementing electronics with a traditional sunshot. *Author*

Below:
The Field Satcom system – along the road to instant, real-time information and intelligence relay.

Right:
It will never fly – but others will because of it: airfield repair by 48 Field Engineer unit at Gutersloh.
Crown copyright photo by SAC Pete Boardman

Below right:
Clean Work – Laser Bay. Immaculate for inspection all the time in the Laser Bay at RAF Bruggen.

our friends in the area, a gesture of support to our United States allies and a cautionary signal to Moscow. Moreover, because of their basic qualities of speed and flexibility, those same aircraft could project British interest in a matter of hours across the entire arc of crisis from Oman to Pakistan, emphasising that their influence is commensurate with their radius of action.

Nor need the application of air power be warlike. In 1979, for example, the Rhodesian settlement was facilitated by the speed with which aircraft could fly in the adminis-

trators and drop supplies to the ex-guerrillas after they had come in from the Rhodesian bush. In fact, without air power the settlement could not have been reached and agreed in the desired timescale.

The traditional gunboat of the 19th century influenced the government and those few citizens who could see it. A modern military aircraft is at once a symbol of technological superiority, a manifestation of a government's military strength and, if deployed by a friendly power, a reassuring token of support which can be made visible over a very wide geographical area to several hundred thousand citizens. In 1985 there are few areas in the world where the interests of the super-powers are not in contention, but each is extremely cautious about risking a serious direct confrontation with the other. Consequently, in any local instability or crisis, there is a great premium on swift, limited military action to pre-empt, stabilize or modify a political situation to the greater advantage of one's own policy and that of one's local friends. Increasingly, the peacetime role of air power is to offer the statesman long range, high speed and multi-directional military support for foreign policy projected to all parts of the globe. It has a deterrent effect not only in the central super-powers confrontation but wherever there may be localised conflict beyond the Tropic of Cancer.

Although not possessing the numbers of the air forces of the two super-powers, the Royal Air Force is equipped to discharge all the roles required of either the Alliance Commanders-in-Chief in wartime or of our statesmen in pracetime. Those roles, and the aircraft and manpower deployed to discharge them, will be examined in subsequent chapters.

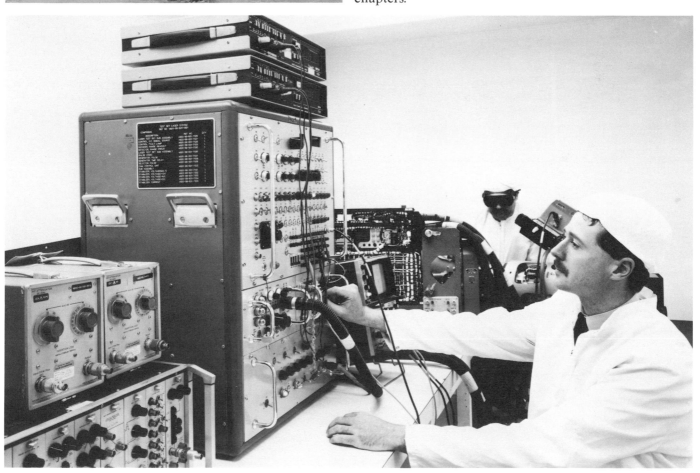

3 Air Defence

In May 1983 Air Chief Marshal Sir Keith Williamson concluded an address to the Royal Society of Arts with the assertion: '... the defence of the United Kingdom base must always be the first charge on any Government.' He had just explained how it had taken Britain nearly 30 years to recover from the self-inflicted wounds of the 1957 Defence White Paper which had included the statement:

'Work will proceed on the development of a ground-to-air missile defence system which will in due course replace the manned aircraft of Fighter Command. In view of the progress already made, the Government have come to the conclusion that the RAF is unlikely to have a requirement for fighter aircraft types more advanced than the supersonic P1, and work on such projects will stop.'

It is not only hindsight which alleges that after the pendulum of offence and defence has swung throughout military history in response to advancing technology it was courting ultimate strategic disaster to attempt to lock it in one place in 1957. As has already been explained in Chapter 1, the concept of the command of the air is as old as air power itself. Twentieth century warfare, up to the conflicts in the Falklands and the Bekaa Valley, has demonstrated that without mastery of one's own airspace, strategies on land and sea are doomed to failure. A fundamental task of British air power in 1985 is to maintain that mastery, over the United Kingdom, in allied European airspace, and further afield in the South Atlantic.

Air Marshal Sir Peter Harding, Vice Chief of the Air Staff in 1984 and previously AOC No 11 Group, observed that 'Air Defence by itself cannot win a war, but it could well prevent its loss. This is especially so when the airspace to be defended is over a key strategic area. Clearly in the content of the strategy of NATO, the United Kingdom is just such an area ...'

In 1940, the air defence of the UK was critical not only to the security of the country, but ultimately to the fate of occupied Europe. Had the RAF lost the Battle of Britain and had the British Isles subsequently been invaded successfully, there would have been no western springboard from which to liberate the allies; no threat to Hitler's western flank as he turned to pursue his eastern ambitions. Instead, from below the shelter provided first by Fighter Command and then by allied air forces, the invasion of Europe was planned and mounted, and Bomber Command and the USAAF launched their offensive against Hitler's own heartland. The loss of the war in 1940 was prevented, and the secure base prepared for the ultimate achievement of victory.

Almost 50 years later, although the country thankfully remained at peace, the air defence of the UK again lay at the heart of the nation's security. In the interim, much had changed. The threat now came from a military machine many times more powerful than any commanded by Hitler: that of the Soviet Union, steadily growing in strength since the end of World War 2 but accelerating even more during the 1970s. Thanks to the North Atlantic alliance Britain did not stand alone but, on the other hand, the potential aggressor no longer had to occupy Western European airfields to come within attacking range.

The Changing Threat

In the early 1950s the major air threat to the UK came from the first generation of postwar Soviet bombers armed with free-fall conventional or nuclear weapons. The squadrons of Fighter Command were deployed on many bases round the British coast from Leuchars in the north to Tangmere in the south, very much as they had been 10 years previously in World War 2. Then, as NATO strategy was modified to deter or to fight a short nuclear war, and as the Soviet Union itself began to deploy surface-to-surface missiles with nuclear warheads, the perception of the threat to the UK changed accordingly. The Defence White Paper of 1957 asserted that the manned bomber would be superseded by the surface-to-surface missile (hence the lack of need to replace the Lightning fighter by

Below:
Close scrutiny of the Sidewinders on a No 23 Squadron Phantom at RAF Stanley by Wg Cdr Peter Langham – the Squadron CO – and the author.

any other manned interceptor), that there was no defence against missile attack, that our defence posture would be based much more exclusively on the nuclear deterrent power of the V-Force and that, therefore, the role of Fighter Command would be reduced to that of protecting the V-Force bases. This remained the posture throughout the 1960s and into the 1970s.

The Soviet Union, however, saw the strategic environment somewhat differently. It did, indeed, develop its surface-to-surface nuclear missiles but also continued to introduce new manned bombers capable of in-flight refuelling and equipped with stand-off weapons with both conventional and nuclear warheads. It is now producing some 30 Tu-22M 'Backfire' bombers a year, of which half are entering service with the Soviet Maritime Air Arm and the others with Long Range Aviation, the equivalent of the old Royal Air Force Bomber Command. 'Backfire' is believed to be capable of speeds of Mach 2 at height, carries a bombload in excess of 12,000lb or the air-to-surface 'Kitchen' long-range stand-off missile, and with in-flight refuelling could attack the United Kingdom from any direction. In the longer term it could be escorted by either later marks of the MiG-23 'Flogger' interceptor or by the longer range two-seat MiG-31 'Foxhound', albeit the latter would be heavily dependent on in-flight refuelling.

Nor is 'Backfire' the only threat. Large numbers of Su-24 'Fencer' are entering service with Frontal Aviation at the rate of 50 a year. From their permanent bases in Western Russia they could reach the UK on a high-low-high flight profile, but if deployed forward to bases in Eastern Germany, they could significantly increase the threat of larger scale low-level attack on these islands. 'Fencer' carries a weapon system specialist seated alongside the pilot to operate the advanced navigation and attack systems which would allow it to fly at low level at night or in bad weather, with a bombload significantly larger than its shorter range predecessors in the Warsaw Pact air forces.

In 1983 the development of a new Soviet bomber, designated 'Blackjack-A' by NATO, was confirmed. 'Blackjack' is larger than the USAF B-1, has a variable geometry wing, and will be capable of long range subsonic cruise, supersonic high altitude dash and low level penetration near the speed of sound. It is expected to be able to drop freefall bombs or launch long range stand-off missiles – perhaps the 2,000km range cruise missile also under development in the USSR. 'Blackjack' could be in service by 1987.

All air attacks on the UK could moreover be expected to be accompanied by powerful electronic warfare support. Some bombers would carry self-screening equipment; some, carrying only jamming equipment, would act as escorts; while others would 'stand off' further away from the bomber streams to give a blanket coverage across a larger area.

Quite clearly therefore the air threat to the UK, and the attendant responsibility of No 11 Group of RAF Strike Command, is likely to increase and become more complex rather than diminish during the next decade. Nor is there any prospect of No 11 Group overlooking its responsibility, because the Soviet maritime and long range air forces offer reminders four or five times a week. Round the North Cape, down through the Iceland–Faroes gap, usually in pairs, come the Tu-95 'Bear-Ds' and 'Bear-Fs' to probe the edges of the British Air Defence Region. The response is swift from the Phantoms and Lightnings maintaining round-the-clock alert at several No 11 Group airfields. The interceptors scramble, climb away over the North Sea and make contact with the intruders at ranges up to 800 miles away. The Soviet crews no doubt are monitoring the speed of the British reaction and the accuracy of the

Below:
A fully-armed Phantom FGR2 at Coningsby – four Sparrow and four Sidewinder missiles and an SUU-23A gun pod.

intercepts. If so they will be in no doubt about the high degree of effectiveness to which they are vulnerable and it takes little imagination to envisage the ensuing calculations back in Soviet air force headquarters. Such is the practical detail of conventional deterrence: the regular demonstration of a defensive capability sufficient to make any aggressor assess his chances of success with the utmost caution.

But as in 1940 it is not only the UK itself which is threatened by air attack but, should deterrence ever fail, the entire war-fighting strategy of the alliance. Since 1967 the NATO strategy of flexible and appropriate response to any aggression has implied a conventional phase of warfare to defend allied territory as near to its eastern borders as possible. But such a strategy is threatened by the in-place numerical superiority of Warsaw Pact ground forces. NATO must be able to rely upon significant reinforcement and resupply in a period of tension and in war. Large proportions of the British ground and air forces based in the UK are destined to reinforce the Continent and they need protection both before and during deployment, and at all stages of subsequent resupply. Considerable numbers of UK and Allied aircraft would operate from British bases, and air transport aircraft carrying North American reinforcements would fly into, over and out of the UK en route to Continental Europe.

Below them there would be extensive naval activity and Britain must provide the base for long range maritime patrols, maritime strike/attack and land-based maritime air defence operations so essential to the support of a

significant proportion of SACLANT's and CINCHAN's surface and sub-surface forces, which would be operating in and around UK and Continental waters and beyond. Finally, Britain is the base for the UK Polaris force and a forward base for US SSBNs. The UK therefore provides an opportunity for defence in depth where command, control and communications may be maintained: a pivotal area whose protection from air attack would be a critical ingredient in any successful alliance strategy.

The Air Defence Team
The team which provides the air defence of the UK comprises separate but closely co-ordinated elements: fighter interceptors, in-flight refuelling tankers, AEW

Above left:
Tomorrow's weapons on today's fighter: Sky Flash missiles carried by a Phantom.

Left:
A rare visit by a Binbrook Lightning to Gutersloh.
Crown copyright photo by SAC Pete Boardman

Above:
The supplement to UK air defences: a Hawk T1 carrying Sidewinders on trials.

aircraft, surface-to-air weapons, and the network of ground radar and control units collectively known as the Air Defence Ground Environment or ADGE.

The Interceptors
The peacetime interceptions are made by the seven fighter squadrons of the Group, all bearing famous numbers and proud traditions. Guarding the northern flank and the eastern Atlantic sea routes are the Phantom FG1s of No 43 Squadron: the 'Fighting Cocks'. No 43 has a particular commitment to the air defence of maritime forces in addition to the broader responsibility to UK airspace. In addition to distinguished service in both world wars, the Squadron has a long association with Scotland, being formed at Stirling in 1916. Sharing the airfield at RAF Leuchars is No 111 Squadron, known familiarly as the 'Tremblers', which claimed 94 enemy aircraft destroyed during the Battle of Britain. 'Treble-One', like all the other RAF Phantom squadrons except No 43 Squadron, flies

the FGR2 or F-4M model which may be armed with four air-to-air Sidewinder heat-seeking missiles and four Sparrow radar-guided longer range missiles as well as a six barrelled General Electric M-61 gun. The FGR2 has an effective unrefuelled combat radius of some 500 miles with a top speed in excess of Mach 2 at height and over Mach 1 at low level, where its pulse doppler radar aids detection and attack.

Also equipped with FGR2s are No 29 Squadron and No 228 OCU at Coningsby and, guarding East Anglia and the approaches to the Home Counties, are Nos 74 and 56 Squadrons at Wattisham. No 74 is equipped with ex-US Navy F-4Js bought to replace the aircraft of No 23 Squadron now permanently based at RAF Stanley. No 29 has been in the night and all-weather fighter game since flying Blenheims at the outbreak of World War 2. No 56, on the other hand, has always hitherto been a day-fighter squadron, including among its World War 1 aircrew Victoria Cross winners Albert Ball and J. B. McCudden, and subsequently playing a prominent part in the Battle of Britain.

The other two squadrons, based at Binbrook in Lincoln-shire, are Nos 5 and 11 Lightning Squadrons which share the task of the Southern Quick Reaction Alert Force with the Wattisham Phantoms. No 5 Squadron forced down the first enemy aircraft of World War 1 on 24 August 1914, while No 11 has had a varied record of service, reverting in 1948 to its original fighter role. The Lightning has now seen 25 years in service and it remains a formidable interceptor. Both squadrons operate a mix of F3 and F6 models and the latter is capable of speeds in excess of

Mach 2. It is equipped with a long range search radar and Red Top missiles which can attack from any angle. For closer range operations it carries two 30mm cannon. Originally designed for high-level operating, the Lightning continues to prove its versatility by intercepting targets at all altitudes and continues to capitalise on its very high speed and high rate of climb.

The level of combat effectiveness achieved by the interceptors of No 11 Group is the product of hard training and a great deal of teamwork. Day to day training will include practice interceptions which will steadily increase in complexity against targets flying at different heights and speeds, sometimes evading, sometimes not, and sometimes against a background of electronic countermeasures. In the Phantom squadrons, teamwork begins with pilot and navigator – the latter not only contributing to the overall lookout but operating the aircraft's own target radar which in the event of heavy enemy jamming of the ground radar station could allow the interception still to be carried out. All the fighter squadrons are likely to spend a great deal of time well away from land in a potentially hostile environment, frequently at low level, and they have not only to locate and intercept a target but also navigate back to base. Nor is the weather of the North Sea and the Iceland–Faroes Gap conducive to visual navigation.

Closer to home however, other aircraft designed originally for clear weather operations have been blended into the interceptor team. Two squadrons of BAe Hawks, normally used to convert fast-jet pilots from basic flying training to their ultimate operational tasks, together with a handful of Hunters can be deployed to operate with radar-equipped fighters in 'mixed fighter force' operations. The Hawks will be armed with AIM-9L Sidewinder missiles and their numbers will in due course be increased. They will augment defences closer to the British coast and provide additional inland 'point' cover when dispersed to airfields throughout the UK.

In the not too distant future however, the Hawks will not be flying so much with Phantoms, as with the Tornado F2 – the air defence variant of the international multi-role combat aircraft already in RAF service in its interdictor strike (IDS) role. A total of 165 Tornado F2s will ultimately replace all the Royal Air Force's Phantoms and Lightnings both in the UK and in Royal Air Force Germany. Full-scale development of the F2 was authorised by the British government in March 1976, and it is scheduled to enter service in 1985. The first two operational conversion trainers were scheduled to fly in early 1984 from Boscombe Down prior to the first production delivery to the RAF 12 months later.

The F2 will be called upon to operate for extended periods on combat patrols over an area stretching from the North Eastern Atlantic, across the North Sea to the mouth of the Baltic, down to the English Channel and, in addition, to contribute towards the air defence of the Central Region of Europe. In those areas it will not only be protecting approaches to the UK but covering Allied maritime forces below it. Finally, it must be able to get airborne from damaged runways.

Tornado F2

The Tornado F2 is the result of the Ministry of Defence's Air Staff Target 395 for a fighter interceptor for the UK Air Defence Region and for Fleet protection. The RAF will have 165 F2s in service by 1990, and these will replace the Lightnings and Phantoms in the air defence role.

Top left:
The first Tornado F2 prototype, ZA254, carrying four Sky Flash and two Sidewinder AAMs, and two long-range fuel tanks. *BAe*

Above left:
ZA254 with wings swept back fully. *BAe*

Above:
Tornado F2 with everything down and four Sky Flash visible.

Below:
Tornado F2 visiting RAF Coningsby, with the new HAS complex in the background.

The production model F2 will be powered by uprated RB199-34R-04 turbofan engines at present installed in the IDS Tornado. Each engine possesses about 8,000lb static thrust raised to 15,000lb with reheat. The F2's fuselage is slightly larger than the IDS to accommodate the nose radome and four Sky Flash missiles. However, the extension has provided additional space for avionics and fuel as well as permitting further improvements to aerodynamic performance. Its basic operational radius of 400 miles will be extended by in-flight refuelling and its supersonic acceleration will be superior to that of the IDS.

As well as the four Sky Flash air-to-air guided missiles, F2 will carry four Raytheon AIM-9L Sidewinders on underwing pylons and a Mauser 27mm cannon recessed in the starboard fuselage. An integral part of the complete weapon system is the new Marconi airborne interceptor radar named Foxhunter. The radar operates in the 3cm Ib band and uses pulse doppler techniques described by Marconi as Frequency Modulated Intermittent Continuous Wave. It carries a wide range of electronic countermeasure features and can track a number of targets simultaneously

at a detection range in excess of 100 miles. The Sky Flash missile itself will be able to engage targets at a distance of 25 miles at very low level and can both discriminate between closely bunched targets and isolate them from background earth clutter. By the end of 1983 several Sky Flash missiles had been successfully fired at both subsonic and supersonic speeds on the prototype aircraft passed through the hands of RAF test crews at Boscombe Down.

Tactical implications of the F2's advanced equipment are considerable. The integration of the aircraft's weapons management and information display systems will permit the crew to respond to directions from the airborne early warning aircraft or the ground without speech transmissions and, because of their full awareness of their immediate tactical environment, to act independently of any external control if circumstances should demand it. As long as external communications do remain open, the aircraft will be able to receive real-time information on unidentified aircraft and jamming sources which will permit the swiftest and most economic allocation of fighter resources where they are most needed. Thus the highest degree of centralised guidance may be safely and simply co-ordinated with a considerable amount of autonomous operation.

The ability to identify enemy aircraft in time to derive the greatest benefit from the weapons systems will be helped not just by the data links with other units in the defence organisation, but by equipment carried by the F2 itself. The IFF interrogator will be valuable, but like any other IFF system will be vulnerable to spoofing and other electronic countermeasures in war. Until ECM-resistant equipment is designed, further reliance will be placed on a

visual augmentation system which is a low light TV camera to allow clear air identification by day and night. In addition, the Radar Homing and Warning Receiver is primarily designed to give the crew visual and audio warning of imminent threats. This equipment, however, will obviously assist identification by distinguishing between signals emitted by hostile and friendly radars.

The final advantage, shared by the F2 with the GR1, is its ability to operate with full weapon and fuel load from less than 1,000yd of concrete. With its integral auxiliary power unit, on-board unserviceability identification and diagnosis systems, and secure, comprehensive communications net, the F2 can be dispersed well away from its home base provided it has access to fuel, weapons and ground crew. Indeed, the advent of the F2 into No 11 Group will present a challenge to the imagination of its operators to ensure that the aircraft's enormous potential is realised fully.

In the longer term, just as the AIM-9L has replaced earlier marks of Sidewinder, so Sky Flash will be replaced by a new international collaborative radar-guided medium range air-to-air weapon, and Sidewinder itself by a short range heat-seeking weapon. It is envisaged that NATO will collaborate on procuring both weapons, with the United States taking the lead in the longer range equipment, and a European consortium, including the United Kingdom, being responsible for the infra-red weapon.

In December 1981 the Hughes Aircraft Corporation was awarded the contract for the medium range air-to-air missile (AMRAAM). Designated AIM-120 it will become the NATO standard beyond visual range air-to-air missile and the primary weapon of the Tornado F2. AIM-120 was designed to meet a specification for a missile which could

AEW

The need for adequate warning of low level intrusion into the UK Air Defence Region by aircraft which could attack from almost any direction led first to the introduction of AEW Shackletons and then to the development of the Nimrod AEW Mk 3.

Above left:
AEW Nimrod XZ286. The distinctive nose and tail radomes contain the scanners for the Marconi Avionics – developed radar system. *BAe*

Above:
A duck-billed Nimrod? A rare but very effective bird.
Crown copyright photo by Sgt Brian Lawrence

Below:
. . . meanwhile, the AEW Shackletons of No 8 Squadron hold the ring, here operating from a forward base at Macrihanish.

be 'fired and forgotten' allowing the interceptor to engage several targets simultaneously, beyond visual range, and which could attack targets regardless of their aspect, altitude or manoeuvres with an all-weather 'look down/ shoot down' capability even in a hostile electronic environment. AIM-120 is faster and lighter than Sky Flash and has three distinct guidance phases: command inertial, autonomous inertial and active terminal. Command inertial mid-course guidance allows up to eight AMRAAMS to be guided simultaneously to eight different targets. If the enemy is using self-screening ECM the missile can be launched on to mid-course and terminal radar home-or-jam guidance. By the end of 1983 AMRAAM had several successful test firings behind it and was moving well towards production in 1984. The Tornado F2 will ultimately carry six AIM-120s, four under the fuselage and two on rails below the wings, as well as retaining the ability to carry Sky Flash.

Early Warning
The impact of the 'Chain Home' early warning radar stations on the course of the Battle of Britain has passed into history. Then, Heinkel and Dornier could be expected to approach from the east at speeds of little more than 200mph. In a future conflict RAF interceptors could face superior numbers at speeds of Mach 2 attacking from both north and west as well as east. The traditional importance of being able to concentrate interceptors at the right place at the right time is therefore likely to remain in any future battle for control of British airspace. But strategic and economic decisions in the 1950s took their toll of British radar cover as well as of the manned interceptor. During the 1960s, many stations, especially those with shorter range, lower level responsibilities were closed down as the Soviet threat was percevied to stem from ballistic missiles rather than conventional bombers.

The USSR however, and not for the first time, perceived the greater flexibility of the manned aircraft as a complement to the apparently unstoppable surface-to-surface missile. By 1970 the new generation of Soviet bombers and fighter-bombers was under development – by 1972 the low-level threat to the UK was becoming apparent. Existing ground radar stations provided good medium and high level cover but below that there were gaps. Consequently No 8 Squadron, itself possessing a famous fighter ground-attack history in both world wars and thereafter, was re-formed with Shackleton AEW2 aircraft, converted from the maritime reconnaissance role as they were replaced by the Nimrod. At its base at Lossiemouth in Northern

Scotland, No 8 Squadron mounted a quick reaction alert, in harness with its faster intereceptor team-mates. On receipt of the news that a 'Bear' was on its way from its lair in the Kola peninsula the QRA Shackleton scrambled with an alacrity that belied its years of service. The endurance that was provided originally to allow it to patrol for 10 hours or more over the Atlantic now permitted it to remain on station for several hours working with the interceptor crews, the sustaining tankers and the ground control unit, providing warning of low-level intrusion far earlier than would be achieved by the ground unit itself and, when required, contributing to the actual control of the interceptors themselves.

But the Shackleton was only a stop-gap as the Soviet threat perceptibly increased. The ability of the bombers to launch weapons several hundred miles away from Britain made it essential that our airborne coverage should be extended even further out over the oceans, while the increasing electronic defences carried by and supporting the bombers meant that the early warning aircraft needed ever more sophisticated equipment to counter them. The crews of No 8 Squadron held the ring tightly but more was required than an aircraft and radars which still had their roots in World War 2.

Originally, the British government had intended to join with NATO in an Alliance purchase of a number of United States E-3 Sentry airborne warning and control (AWAC) aircraft but lengthy delays in the ability of the Allies to agree the conditions of such a purchase led to the British decision in March 1977 to develop the Nimrod airframe and engines as a national AEW aircraft. It was believed that any further delay in preparing the replace-

ment for the Shackleton would leave a serious gap in the UK air defence system. The first Nimrod AEW squadron formed at RAF Waddington in 1984 inheriting the illustrious number plate of No 8 Squadon.

Nimrod AEW3 is readily distinguishable from its maritime predecessors by the bulbous radomes mounted on the nose and tail. In wing-tip pods it carries electronic support measures equipment. Not surprisingly, it has been described as 'a flying radar station'. Two Ferranti FIN-1012 inertial navigation platforms provide the information about the aircraft's own position, heading and attitude which must be absolutely accurate so that the rest of the system may be reliable. Its function is to complement ground-based radars by extending coverage much further away from the United Kingdom's coastline and to much lower levels. Nimrod will provide early warning information to the air defence network and should ground control units be eliminated from the conflict, it could control fighters directly itself. Unlike AWACS, however, it is not designed to provide an alternative airborne control post for offensive operations.

The aircraft will use three methods to detect and clarify targets. First is the pulse doppler radar which operates in

Right:
A dramatic view of the aerodynamic impact of AEW Nimrod's forward radome.

Below:
Stranger in the night: an AEW Nimrod is taken into protective custody during a visit to RAF Cottesmore.
Crown Copyright photo by Sgt Brian Lawrence

VC10 K2 ZA141 prepares to refuel two Phantoms during combined services AAR trials in 1983. The five ex-Gulf Air standard VC10s converted to K2 standard can carry 75 tonnes of fuel, and will be joined in service by at least four of the Super VC10 K3 conversions.

two modes: high pulse repetition frequency for tracking fast moving targets, and a lower range which would identify slow moving objects such as ships. The radar's extensive electronic counter countermeasures protection will be enhanced by frequency agility. The second method of detection is the IFF interrogator which is co-ordinated with the radar response reception; and the third, the electronic support measures equipment which automatically compares emissions received with those stored in its memory bank. Communication with other elements in the air defence ground environment, AWACS and Royal Navy ships will initially be by NATO data link 11 and, subsequently, by the highly secure joint tactical information distribution system (JTIDS).

The Nimrod AEW force will ultimately comprise 11 aircraft, flying from their peacetime base at Waddington but readily deployable in times of tension or actual conflict to forward operating bases at either end of the country, such as St Mawgan or Kinloss. Thus Nimrod AEW adds a further dimension to UK defence. An unhappy memory in British military history is the dependence of Singapore on fixed defences facing out to sea which were taken quickly in the flank by Japanese forces attacking from the Malayan peninsula. Such is the flexibility of air defence, amplified by Nimrod, that the defences of the UK could be switched from Northern Scotland to Southern England in a very small number of hours, thereby closing the back door as effectively as the front.

The Supporting Tankers
In the last decade another expression has entered the air power vocabulary: the force-multiplier. In one sense, any innovation or improvement which promotes greater effectiveness of man or equipment is a force-multiplier, but the term may be most aptly used to describe the contribution to air operations of in-flight refuelling.

Photographs of Victors refuelling Lightnings, Phantoms, Buccaneers, Hercules and Nimrods are now commonplace. Indeed, the early months of the airbridge to the

Falklands would have been impossible without not only the Victor K2s but also the hastily converted Hercules C1Ks. Only since 1972 however have the RAF's air defence interceptors been able to call upon in-flight, or air-to-air, refuelling. Prior to that date they were limited in range and duration on patrol by the amount of fuel they could lift off with them. They had little ability to loiter ahead of an incoming raid or to switch to another set of targets after engaging the first. Now however the Phantoms and Lightnings, and in the near future the Tornado F2s, can mount combat air patrols (CAP) many hundreds of miles from base. They can intercept a hostile aircraft before its own missile release point, and with remaining weapons be vectored against others perhaps several hundred miles away on different tracks. The patrol limitations become crew fatigue rather than fuel; the combat limitations may be spent weapons rather than either. In practical terms a CAP can now be sustained between Iceland and Norway: a far cry from the scramble to intercept the Luftflotten over the Medway.

For over a decade in-flight refuelling support has been given to the air defence fighters by the 21 Victor K2s of Nos 55 and 57 Squadrons from the peacetime base at Marham. Now however, this support has been considerably expanded with the entry into service of No 101 Squadron at Brize Norton. When the Squadron is complete it will fly five VC10 K2s and four Super VC10 K3 tankers, each providing some 25% increase in fuel capacity over the Victors. Moreover, the RAF still holds a further 14 ex-airline VC10s, intended for spares but providing for further expansion of the tanker fleet if priorities were to be

35

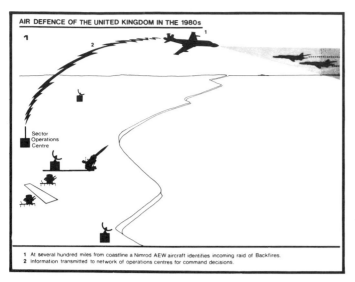

AIR DEFENCE OF THE UNITED KINGDOM IN THE 1980s

Sector Operations Centre

1 At several hundred miles from coastline a Nimrod AEW aircraft identifies incoming raid of Backfires.
2 Information transmitted to network of operations centres for command decisions.

so assessed. Finally, the purchase in 1982 of six ex-British Airways Lockheed Tristar 500s for possible multi-role transport/tanker use offers still further promise of refuelling support.

Surface-to-Air Defences

For those enemy aircraft which might evade the manned interceptors, a second line of defence awaits. By no means all Soviet aircraft are likely to be equipped with stand-off missiles. Those with freefall weapons must overfly their targets, ideally from their point of view at high speed and low level to reduce their vulnerability to ground fire. In the age of the surface-to-air missile (SAM) that vulnerability has been considerably increased over the UK by the deployment of Bloodhound and Rapier systems.

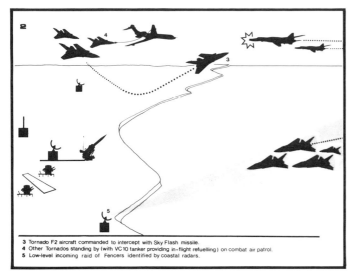

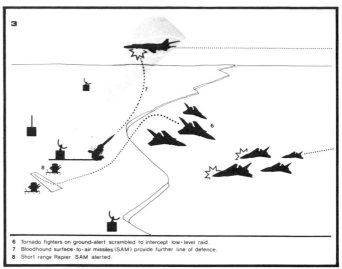

3 Tornado F2 aircraft commanded to intercept with Sky Flash missile.
4 Other Tornados standing by (with VC 10 tanker providing in-flight refuelling) on combat air patrol.
5 Low-level incoming raid of Fencers identified by coastal radars.

6 Tornado fighters on ground-alert scrambled to intercept low-level raid.
7 Bloodhound surface-to-air missiles (SAM) provide further line of defence.
8 Short range Rapier SAM alerted.

Bloodhound is an older system, the current Mk 2 entering RAF service in 1964 but still effective at medium and low levels. Radar guided and powered by four solid propellant motors its high explosive proximity-fused warhead is lethal at heights from 100 to more than 60,000ft. As part of a general reorganisation of NATO air defences, No 85 Squadron in the UK was joined in 1982 by units of No 25 Squadron from Germany to increase defensive coverage of Lincolnshire and East Anglia.

It is however the deployment of the British Aerospace Rapier which presents attacking formations with their most difficult low level SAM problem in UK airspace. Rapier is the outcome of a NATO requirement for a low level air defence system to replace guns and to be capable of knocking out aircraft before they can reach a position to launch a stand-off weapon. It is a comparatively light-weight, low cost, highly mobile system, originally developed in competition with the US MAULER system, which was subsequently cancelled.

The principal components of the Rapier system are the launcher and tracker. The launcher carries four rounds on a turntable, the command link computer and antenna, and a surveillance radar with IFF interrogator. The radar antenna rotates once every second, providing warning of incoming aircraft so that they can be acquired by the tracking system at the earliest possible moment. In its basic daylight defence version, the target is tracked optically, the operator using a small joystick to hold the aiming mark on the centre of mass of the aircraft. A TV tracker that moves with the optical sight head auto-matically measures the offset of the flares on the Rapier missile from the line of sight, and the computer generates corrective signals, which are fed to the missile from the command antenna on the launcher.

The system is modular, allowing the addition of a Marconi DN181 Blindfire radar tracker, which provides all-weather day/night capability. Blindfire generates a very narrow pencil beam, separately tracking the target and missile, and feeding error measurements to the command guidance computer in the same way as the TV tracker of the optical system. The manufacturer claims a single-shot kill probability of around 90% with Blindfire compared with perhaps 75% for the basic optical tracker.

Rapier has been in operation with RAF Regiment squadrons since 1974. It is a short-range, highly effective low-level rapid reaction weapon which, although normally deployed for point protection such as airfields, is highly mobile, each unit requiring only three Land Rovers. Typical of such a squadron is No 27 Rapier Squadron RAF Regiment, equipped with the Blindfire target acquisition system which provides 24-hour air-to-surface defence at RAF Leuchars. Further north, No 48 Squadron defends the approaches to the Moray Firth, while as a result of a bilateral agreement several USAF bases in England are also to be defended by Rapier. The first squadron formed in 1983 and two others are following in 1984 and 1986.

Unlike Bloodhound, the Rapier is a 'hittile'. Bloodhound was designed for use against aircraft unlikely to be close to any friendly forces or ground equipment and therefore the

Top left:
Bloodhound surface-to-air missiles of No 25 Squadron, at RAF Wildenrath, now redeployed to East Anglia.

Left:
An unwelcome sight for an Argentinian pilot – the launch of a Rapier missile. On this occasion a live round but on the practice range at Benbecula.
Crown copyright photo by SAC Pete Boardman

Above:
Rapier Blindfire radar in the Falkland Islands, and the author emerging from the well-concealed dugout of the missile battery's crew.

proximity fuse was well suited for use in it. For use against very low flying aircraft however, there must be no risk of premature or 'diverted' detonation and thus Rapier is in essence a 42.6kg round of ammunition. The manufactures claim that the surveillance radar provides a detection range of 8–11.5km, depending on the size of target. The range bracket for the missile is officially quoted as 0.5–7.0km, with a nominal altitude capability of 10,000ft.

For deployment, one Land Rover carries the optical tracker and four missiles, and tows a trailer on which is loaded the launcher and generating set. The second carries a further nine missiles. The third tows the Blindfire radar on a trailer. A Rapier fire unit requires three men to bring it into action, but once established it can be operated by one man if necessary. Reaction time is six seconds in optical or Blindfire mode. Four missiles can be reloaded by two men within 2½ minutes. In the Falklands campaign the weapon is believed to have accounted for 14 Argentine aircraft out of 72 confirmed kills and another six out of the 14 probables destroyed by a total of 13 different weapon systems.

Automatic weapons may have a part to play in airfield defence providing at least a visual deterrent to air attack by virtue of tracer ammunition and shell bursts, but only a guided missile can provide a high kill probability by compensating for target motion, and kill at the ranges needed to defeat (for instance) laser-guided bomb attacks. Obliged to choose one system, the RAF phased out its last gun defence in 1978.

The Ground Environment
Even the most cursory survey of the air threat to the UK and the active defensive resources ranged against it

Readiness

Only rigorous training and the professionalism of all RAF personnel enables the efficient application of air power. To ensure readiness for any eventuality units are tested in competitions, exercises and, most demanding of all, the TACEVAL of a whole station.

Above:
NBC kit: an exercise cameo in a RAF operations room.

Below:
Treating 'casualties' of a chemical attack. For today's RAF the front line begins on one's own airfield.

Right:
Mobile ground defence: a Scorpion of the RAF Regiment sets out to deal with intruders on an exercise.

Below right:
Decontamination after a simulated chemical attack on RAF Coningsby.

indicates the enormous complexity of actually commanding and controlling those resources in any future conflict. In the UK air defence region at any one time there could be several varieties of hostile aircraft, friendly interceptors, friendly offensive aircraft transiting to or from a European combat zone, friendly transport aircraft, tankers, AEW aircraft and possibly even very uncomfortable neutral civil aircraft. Below them all the missile operators, acutely conscious that an error of identification on their part could prove lethal either to their coleagues or to themselves. The whole view is likely to be distorted by electronic warfare.

The system which must impose order on that potential chaos is known as the UK Air Defence Ground Environment (UKADGE) and its requirements are readily stated. It must be able to give the earliest warning of impending attack, to distinguish friend from foe, to quantify attacks, to communicate swiftly with all defensive element, to concentrate forces, to redeploy, to reinforce, to defy electronic distortion and to survive physical attack. These tasks will become even more complex as the low level, stand-off and electronic warfare capability of the enemy continues to grow. Margins of error will continue to reduce as our own surface-to-air defences increase their responsiveness and lethality.

The need to modernise the UKADGE to meet these requirements was comprehensively forecast by a specialist Air Defence Environment Team report and, after several lean financial years for defence, in 1980 a five-year £150million programme to improve the UKADGE was begun. When complete it will provide radar coverage over four million square miles extending to 1,000 miles from Britain's coasts. It will include new mobile long range 3D radars, secure and ECM-resistant digital communications links, and automatic data processing and displays. Consequently, not only will the positive value of instantaneous and secure command, control and communication between all allied units be achieved but an enemy will not be able to paralyse or destroy the system by attacking any one component. The potential disasters in 1940 of the loss of a Kenley control centre or an Isle of Wight radar should not be a threat in a future air battle in British airspace.

Readiness
The ability of two RAF Phantoms to drop down alongside an inquisitive 'Bear' out over northern waters, demon-

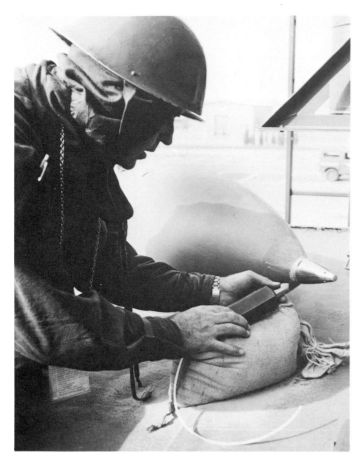

Left:
Fitting Sidewinders.

Above:
Loading an SUU-23 gun pod during exercise.

Above left:
Bomb disposal during exercise at Bruggen. *Crown copyright photo by Sgt Don Lambert*

Right:
Now you see him, now you don't . . . The fighter combat simulator at British Aerospace's Warton Division. *BAe*

strating a further ability to take more drastic action should the need arise, is the product of long hours of rigorous training by the aircrew, matched by equal professionalism among the many hundreds of airmen and airwomen in other parts of the overall system. Routine training, therefore, involves all-weather practice interceptions, QRA, working with the Nimrods, in-flight refuelling, mastering procedures with the surface-to-air missile squadrons, flying almost instinctively with ground control and confidently without it. Indeed, such training can scarcely be called routine, yet compared to other activities it may well seem to be so to the fighter crews.

For several years now the USAF has maintained at RAF Alconbury an 'Aggressor' squadron of F-5s whose task is to provide 'dissimilar' combat training to USAF and RAF fighter crews. Obviously, when the majority of peacetime RAF 'interceptions' are made against friendly Phantoms there are the obvious dangers of combat parameters becoming determined by the similarity of the aircraft themselves. The lightweight F-5, however, can be flown in very different patterns thereby greatly extending the range of threats to which the RAF crews can become accustomed. Inevitably, keen but good-humoured Allied rivalry gives added spice to the encounters.

A further diversion occurs when the squadrons move away to overseas bases for additional training or competitions. The Mediterranean, for example, might not always present the operational challenges of the North Sea environment but there are obvious compensations in the guaranteed clear weather for those exercises which depend on visual target acquisition and clear air manoeuvres. In October 1980 Gp Capt Alan Parkes, Station Commander at Akrotiri in Cyprus, explained how his unit provided facilities for the squadrons of No 11 Group:

'We are busy for some 10 months of the year with these Armament Practice Camps. Each squadron comes here for about five weeks and carries out its annual training with live gunfire. The target-towing aircraft are Canberras of 100 Squadron. Each fighter pilot flies a number of cine-camera sorties until he has demonstrated that he can consistently achieve the required safety parameters of range and angle-off, chasing the Canberra towing a target banner on a 300 yd rope. The Squadron Weapons Instructor then tests the pilot firing live 30mm shells against the banner. The pilot then flies six academic shoots in order to gain Allied Command Europe qualifications. This qualification is a percentage score based on hits made against

rounds fired and the standard, laid down by Supreme Headquarters Allied Powers Europe, is common to all NATO Air Forces.'

Closer to home, regular missile-firing practice takes place at ranges off North Wales and Northeastern Scotland while squadron exchanges with NATO allies encourage both competition and an awareness of common procedure and objectives.

The most realistic training of all, however, occurs when the entire station assumes that actual conflict has started and, under the eagle eyes of Allied Staff Officers, the squadrons demonstrate how effectively they can operate under simulated wartime conditions. Such conditions may be applied to one station only – which is called a Tactical Evaluation or TACEVAL for short – or it may be part of No 11 Group or regular NATO-wide defence exercises.

TACEVAL is the test by SACEUR of a station's ability to move swiftly from peacetime to war conditions and of its capacity to fight a war. The Evaluation Team will simulate just about every incident that could disrupt the air defence task. Aircraft will be declared destroyed on the ground, runways will be obstructed, fuel installations fired, the station commander or any combination of his deputies 'killed', a chemical attack received, all communications jammed; and yet the fighters must get airborne and the interceptions made. At the end of the exercise the performance of the squadrons will be assessed and it is a considerable source of pride among units of No 11 Group, as indeed elsewhere in the Royal Air Force, that standards achieved are consistently well above the NATO average.

If the station is participating in a broader NATO exercise, more offensive and defensive resources of the Alliance will be drawn upon. Such was the case in April 1980 when, for three days, No 11 Group was subjected to repeated attacks by aircraft from the United States, German, Canadian, Netherlands, Norwegian, Belgian and French Air Forces. The Lightnings and Phantoms of the seven fighter squadrons were supplemented as they would be in actual conflict by the Lightnings of the Lightning Training Flight at Binbrook, the Phantoms of No 228 OCU at Coningsby and the Hawks and Hunters from the No 11 Group tactical Weapons Units at Brawdy and Lossiemouth. Alliance solidarity was confirmed by the commitment to the defence of the UK by USAF F-15s and F-5s which reflected their likely wartime roles. Altogether, some 100 aircraft defended UK airspace against 300 aggressors. On the ground, air bases were defended by the RAF Regiment against 'diversionary brigades' or 'saboteurs', the Royal Observer Corps was deployed and Bloodhound and Rapier units were exercised.

Royal Air Force Wattisham was opened to the national press for the third day of the exercise, which began with a low-level attack by six Luftwaffe F-4K Phantoms, followed quickly by four F-104 Starfighters of the Royal Canadian Air Force. Synchronised with the attacks, ground explosions were detonated and the passive defence units of the station had to cope with fires and 'casualties' while full operational response was being maintained by the squadrons. A more sinister attack was made by a lone aggressor Hunter which, in a single highspeed low-level pass, simulated a chemical attack but, thoroughly drilled in many station exercises, all ground personnel had

already donned their nuclear biological and chemical dress and still the Phantoms of Nos 56 and 23 Squadrons continued to get airborne. Finally, by the end of one 36-hour period the two squadrons alone had made almost 200 interceptions. As Air Vice Marshal Peter Latham AOC No 11 Group observed, 'Most excellent. Britain's air defence is the very best we can do with our resources. We have a highly skilled force with very good equipment.'

Forward Air Defence

It is idle to speculate now on the defensive implications for the RAF in 1940 if the German armies had not overrun France, the Low Countries and Norway, thereby bringing the British Isles within striking distance of the medium range bombers of the Luftwaffe. We could, as we had expected before 1939, have relied on forward air defences over the continent to provide an additional barrier to enemy bombers if not keep them out of range altogether.

In 1985, as has already been explained, the Warsaw Pact light and medium bomber forces could reach the British Isles from their existing bases while the 'heavies' have the range to attack from the northwest. Nevertheless, forward air defence over Western Europe is at least as important now as in 1939 and, in some respects, infinitely more

challenging. At the beginning of this decade the Warsaw Pact deployed almost 2,000 fighter-bombers, 350 bombers, and 700 attack helicopters in the European theatre. In addition, many of the 4,000 interceptor force could be employed in ground attack roles. All were steadily being strengthened either by one for one replacement by new types, as for example Su-24 'Fencer' for Su-17 'Fitter', or by progressive update of radar, engines or weapons. In 1941

Forward Air Defence

The presence of RAF fighter squadrons in Western Germany should be seen not only as part of the UK's commitment to defend the integrity of the Federal German Republic, but also as an essential element in the defence of the UK.

Above:
No 92 Squadron Phantom being pushed back into a hardened shelter at Wildenrath.

Right:
A Phantom of No 43 Squadron wrapped up for the night while visiting Gutersloh.
Crown copyright photo by Cpl Geoff Card

Top:
A Phantom of No 19 Squadron at Wildenrath.

Below:
The defender defended: RAF police dog handler and Phantom in RAFG.

Above:
USAF F-15 Eagle visiting Gutersloh, armed with Sidewinder. The presence of F-15s at RAF bases, and their commitment to UK air defence during exercises, reflects their likely wartime role.

the Soviet Air Force learned a bitter lesson at the hands of the Luftwaffe: Russian sources themselves acknowledge the loss of 1,500 aircraft in the first 24 hours of the war and 6,000 in the first seven days. After taking that lesson to heart modern Soviet combined-arms doctrine lays great stress on the contribution of its own air power in any large scale offensive. The bomber force is expected to smash a gap in Western air defences by destroying early warning radars, surface-to-air missile sites and airfields. Advancing armoured divisions are to be accompanied or preceded by close air support fixed-wing aircraft and helicopters, while other helicopters may be expected to try to place units of Soviet divisionary brigade troops on key points behind NATO forward defences. Forward air defence is not therefore an expensive luxury for the Western allies but an indispensable element in withstanding a Warsaw Pact offensive.

Throughout the RAF there is no lack of understanding of the fact that peacetime preparedness is an indispensable element to deterrence to war, but on units in RAF Germany (RAFG) one becomes conscious very quickly of the proximity of the potential enemy. The Command Headquarters in the forests at Rheindahlen is only 30 minutes 'Flogger' flying time from the Inner German Border (IGB). Gutersloh, on the eastern side of the Rhine, is only half that distance. Consequently, the German bases have been given first priority in the provision of hardened shelters (HAS) for all combat aircraft, and in the 'toning down' programme which has resulted in all buildings, runways and taxiways being painted or treated to give a dull green finish. Stations are encircled with barbed wire and sand-bagged emplacements, to leave no visitor in doubt, as the notice by Bruggen gate has it: 'The task of this Station in peace is to train for war'. The forthright character of the commanding officer who installed this notice is commemorated by the next few words '. . . and don't you forget it'. Such a notice would be appropriate for any base in the RAF.

Wildenrath, on the west bank of the Rhine near Rheindahlen, is the home of Nos 19 and 92 Fighter Squadrons, equipped with Phantom FGR2s. No 19 Squadron has one of the proudest records in the RAF. It accounted for 281 enemy aircraft in World War 1 after its formation on 1 September 1915 and, after being the first squadron to receive the Spitfire in 1938, shot down a further 145 in World War 2. It has been equipped with the

FGR2 Phantom at Wildenrath since January 1977. No 92 Squadron followed No 19 to Wildenrath in April 1977 and it also has a distinguished history. After service in World War I, it was a notable participant in the Battle of Britain, flying from Biggin Hill. Among the famous pilots were Wg Cdr A. G. 'Sailor' Malan and Flt Lt Bob Stanford Tuck. By the end of the war the Squadron had claimed 317½ enemy aircraft destroyed. Now, both squadrons combine in peacetime to carry out a commitment retained by the UK under the terms of the Bonn Convention to defend the integrity of the airspace over the northern half of the Federal Republic of Germany, as well as to contribute to SACEUR's comprehensive air defence provision in the Central Region of Allied Command Europe.

Consequently, like their colleagues in No 11 Group in the UK, the aircrews of Nos 19 and 92 Squadrons maintain aircraft on constant states of immediate readi-

ness to scramble to intercept unidentified aircraft trespassing in the Air Defence Identification Zone, an invisible barrier stretching down the western side of the border with East Germany. Battle Flight is scrambled on average twice a week, sometimes as a practice, sometimes for real. Within seconds of the klaxon's wailing, the two Spey engines with the afterburners in will give the Phantoms 18,000lb of thrust down Wildenrath's runway, yet the crews will not know whether the scramble is a practice called by sector control centre or a response to a real intrusion from across the frontier. In either case they will be armed with four radar-guided Sparrow and four infra-red homing Sidewinder missiles and a 20mm six-barrel cannon able to fire 1,000 rounds a minute. In peacetime they will remain under ground control until the intruder is within range of the aircraft's own all-weather radar. Thereafter, the radar navigator in the back seat will vector the fighter into a position from which the pilot can make a visual identification. Under other conditions, of course, and subject to the rules of engagement in force at the time, the Phantom would be positioned to attack with the appropriate weapon system. So far the culprits have not come from across the border: they are sometimes private aircraft off track or occasionally civilian airliners with a faulty identification transponder. But, whatever their height, speed and type, they are very vulnerable. The combination of long range, look-down, all-weather radar, two-man crew and weapon mix make the FGR2s of Nos 19 and 92 Squadrons formidable opponents at either high or low level. This constant national requirement for the Battle Flight ensures a very high peacetime readiness state which enhances the Squadrons' preparation for their wartime role under SACEUR.

Left:
The Agile Combat Aircraft mock-up at the Paris Air Show in 1983. *BAe*

Below:
The air superiority fighter of the future? A full-scale mock-up of the ACA (Agile Combat Aircraft), an Anglo-German-Italian (British Aerospace, Messerschmitt-Bolkow-Blohm, Aeritalia) project, for service in the 1990s. Weapons shown here include advanced short and medium range air-to-air missiles. *BAe*

In recent years the Warsaw Pact air forces have placed increasing emphasis on lower level offensive operations. While not descending to heights habitually flown by Tornado, Harrier and Jaguar crews, the 'Fitters' and 'Fencers' could be expected at less than 500ft. Consequently a large proportion of the training carried out by the Wildenrath squadrons occurs at low level, placing an even higher premium on navigational and pilot skills. Alongside the RAF Phantoms are ranged the F-15s, F-16s and Phantoms of the other allied air forces. Together they comprise a well trained and well equipped fighter force, which, should ever deterrence fail, they would need to be.

The Surface-to-Air Defences

NATO's air defences are, of course, not dependent on the manned interceptor. The belt of Allied surface-to-air missiles running from the Baltic to the Austrian border, known by its components as the Nike-Hawk system, is complemented by the weapons deployed by RAFG. Short-range, low-level SAM defence is provided by the British Aerospace/Marconi Rapier. During the last decade the offensive aircraft of Frontal Aviation, the tactical arm of the Soviet air forces, have greatly increased their range and payload. Sukhoi Su-17 'Fencer-C', Mikoyan MiG-23 'Flogger-G' and Mikoyan MiG-27 'Flogger-J' now present a qualitative and quantitative low-level threat which was simply not present 10 years ago. In view of the essential contribution which air power must make to NATO strategy, it is to be expected that British airfields will be high priority targets for Warsaw Pact aircraft. If they should penetrate the fighter screen and the Nike-Hawk belt they will be met by four Rapier squadrons of No 4 Wing of the RAF Regiment, one of which is based at Wildenrath and the others at Laarbruch, Bruggen and Gutersloh. Each Rapier squadron has eight fire units with four missiles on line at each unit. The units are fully mobile and quickly dispersed to locations away from the airfields in times of tension, which would permit low-level intercept of high speed attacking aircraft before they reached their missile launch point. Each unit is equipped with Identification Friend or Foe (IFF) systems and the recent addition of the Marconi DM1818 Blindfire radar has added an all-weather and nigh capability to the original optical system.

Future Fighter Development

In looking further ahead to the demands of the European theatre, the Royal Air Force has identified the need for a fighter to contribute to the battle for air superiority. In World War 2 there was little public distinction between the Spitfire as an air superiority fighter and the Spitfire as an interceptor. Since then the demand for a British fighter to be able to scramble, climb rapidly and engage a hostile bomber has been complemented by the need for an aircraft to more than hold its own against the increasingly agile fighters and fighter-bombers of the Warsaw Pact. The Lightning and Phantom, and now Tornado F2, are all excellent interceptors, but not designed for low level, highly manoeuvrable air combat. Consequently, on 16 December 1983 the Chiefs of Staff of the air forces of Great Britain, the Federal Republic of Germany, France, Italy and Spain signed a common military agreement at Wahn air force base in West Germany on the Outline European Staff Target for a future European fighter

aircraft. Several of the desired characteristics of the joint venture were publicised during 1984. It was suggested that the standard air-to-air armament would be six missiles, probably drawn from the new NATO Family of Weapons described below. In addition the fighter will carry at least one gun and will also have an air-to-ground role. It is likely to be twin-engined and be capable of air-to-air refuelling. Its short take-off and landing specification is 500m of runway with full tanks, fully loaded guns and four air-to-air missiles. It is not yet certain whether it will achieve short-field performance by thrust reversal, two-dimensional nozzles or aerodynamic surfaces. In any event it must be able to operate on undeveloped landing areas without ground support. Although specified as a single-seat fighter, a two-seat trainer which must be fully combat capable will also be built. The ECM fit should be integrated in the fuselage, thereby releasing all underwing positions for offensive weapons.

The exact contribution of each nation to the design and production of the European fighter remains to be determined, but the British aerospace industry got away to a flying start with its Agile Combat Aircraft concept deployed in mock-up in 1982. In 1983 the British Ministry of Defence placed a contract with British Aerospace to build a flying technology demonstrator prior to possible funding for large scale operational service. The experimental

Air Defence in the South Atlantic

Above left:
Extended air defence over the Falklands. A Hercules tanker of No 1312 Flight refuels a Harrier GR3 of No 1453 Flight, escorted by Phantoms of No 23 squadron.

Left:
The view from the back door: a Phantom of No 23 Squadron as seen from the refuelling hatch of a Hercules of No 1312 Flight over the Falklands.

Above:
Sidewinder-armed Harriers at RAF Stanley. *Author*

programme will concentrate on the essential attributes of a good air combat fighter: high acceleration, maximum usable lift, sustained turn rates and specific excess power. The ACA will have a single seat, a twin fin, a canard/delta and twin engines. As a demonstrator rather than a prototype it gives opportunity to experiment with several technologies, thereby keeping options open on final design which could be considered in competition for, or part of, the new multinational project, and eventually as the Harrier replacement in the next decade.

It is however impossible to separate the weapon platform from the weapon that it will launch. Indeed, there are good grounds in modern military aircraft design for turning the sequence round: identifying the job to be done, envisaging the desired weapon, and then building the aircraft to carry it. Fortunately, development of EFA and its primary air-to-air weapons will proceed apace. In 1980 a Memorandum of Understanding was signed between the USA, the FRG, and the UK for Britain and West Germany to produce 'an Advanced Short Range Air-to-Air Missile' (ASRAAM) under the NATO Family of Weapons concept which allocates long range (AMRAAM) development to the USA. Engineering development of the weapon is scheduled to begin in 1985. It will employ a passive infra-red seeker, and be used for all angles of attack. The weapon system could be expected to have a multi-target engagement capability and a very high average speed. The combination of new missile and new combat aircraft should maintain the technological superiority which has hitherto played such an important part in offsetting NATO's numerical inferiority in any future air war in Europe.

Air Defence in the South Atlantic

Hopefully the deterrence posture of the Western alliance will continue to ensure that Europe enjoys its longest period of unbroken peace for several hundred years. In 1984 however, a state of war still existed in the South Atlantic. Tentative diplomatic moves by both sides appeared to be reducing the immediate tension over the Falkland Islands issue but the security of the British inhabitants still depended on military defence. In the months after the end of open conflict there were several press reports indicating that the Argentine armed forces were seeking to replace their equipment lost in battle, and working to learn the tactical lessons of their defeat. While the Argentine Air Force had paid dearly for the bravery of its pilots, it was sometimes overlooked that the equally effective naval pilots had not only not lost any Super Etendards, but had steadily brought all 14 of their French purchases into squadron service. The new strategic airfield at Mount Pleasant was still many months from completion, and the British garrison on the Islands was still dependent on the slender airbridge and seaborne supplies.

As the Argentinians had themselves discovered, the tiny group of islands was not easy to defend against air attack. The airfield at Stanley had no natural cover, was very restricted in space, and its outlines, close to an irregular indented coastline, were readily identifiable by radar. Conversely, defensive radar coverage was limited to the two or three quickly located static radars on the two main islands supplemented by picket ships and, later, airborne early warning helicopters. Nevertheless the defensive team which had been assembled by mid-1984 was strong enough to make even a token Argentinian air attack a very risky business.

No 23 Squadron, equipped with Phantom FGR2s, had re-formed at Stanley after previous service at Wattisham. The aircraft carried the standard Phantom weapon fit of four radar-guided Sparrow missiles, four AIM-9L Sidewinders and the six barrelled Gatling gun. Closer to the islands they were supported by Sidewinder-equipped Harrier GR3s which had originally flown out from Wittering. Both could fly extended combat air patrols as a result of the in-flight refuelling supplied by the converted Hercules C Mk 1s also on permanent detachment at Stanley. The combined services' harmony which had proved so successful in combat was preserved in the air by the conversion of two Royal Navy Sea Kings to carry an airborne version of the Thorn EMI Searchwater radar which is an integral part of the Nimrod Mk 2 maritime reconnaissance system. The details of the modification to the radar remain classified, but as the original was designed to detect targets against sea clutter, it is clearly capable of locating aircraft under similar circumstances. The Sea Kings' own combat radius and height combine therefore to give a considerably extended early warning to the air defences. Not only that, the mobility of the helicopters, demonstrating yet again the flexibility of air power, means that no sneak Argentinian attack could ever count on locating and blinding them, thus deterring such a possibility even more. Finally, point defence is provided by Rapier batteries. During the conflict, Rapier units manned by soldiers of No 12 Air Defence Regiment Royal Artillery were credited with 14 confirmed aircraft kills and eight probables, from some 50–60 rounds fired. This high rate of success was achieved despite hasty movement and siting, extremes of environmental conditions and no radar assistance. The current deployments on the other hand are all well positioned, well maintained and equipped with Blindfire radar. All in all, any Argentinian attempt either to attack or retake the Falkland Islands would require an extremely heavy investment in long range offensive air power, quite apart from land and naval resources, to have even the slightest chance of success. Even in a region where sea power has traditionally been the dominant strategic element, air power, and particularly air defence, is now the hinge upon which victory or defeat would turn.

Above right:
Sqn Ldr Richard Thomas, then commanding No 1453 Flight, returns from a combat air patrol over the Falklands in July 1983. *Author*

Right:
Not an alternative to Rapier, but a captured Argentinian armoured car at RAF Stanley. *Author*

Below:
Rapier on guard somewhere in the Falklands. *Author*

4 Strike, Attack and Reconnaissance

Throughout history a strong military defence often discouraged enemy attack but, should he ever overcome his reluctance, he could not normally be defeated by defensive measures alone. A siege could be withstood, a battle could produce a stalemate, a sustained unsuccessful offensive could prove so costly that an attacker could be seriously weakened; but without a counter-offensive the enemy could withdraw without penalty and prepare a further assault.

As in any other medium of warfare, the pendulum of offence and defence has swung backwards and forwards in the air since 1916, when Gen Trenchard sent the following minute to Gen Haig:

'It is sometimes argued that our aeroplanes should be able to prevent hostile aeroplanes from crossing the line, and this idea leads to a demand for defensive measures and a defensive policy. Now is the time to consider whether such a policy would be possible, desirable and successful.

'It is the deliberate opinion of all those most competent to judge, that this is not the case, and that an aeroplane is an offensive and not a defensive weapon. Owing to the unlimited space in the air, the difficulty one machine has in seeing another, the accidents of wind and cloud, it is impossible for aeroplanes, however skilful and vigilant their pilots, however numerous their formations, to prevent hostile aircraft from crossing the line if they have the initiative and determination to do so...

From the accounts of prisoners, we gather that the enemy's aeroplanes received orders not to cross the lines over the French or British front unless the day is cloudy and a surprise attack can be made, presumably in order to avoid unnecessary casualties. On the other hand, British aviation has been guided by a policy of relentless and incessant offensive. Our machines have continually attacked the enemy on his side of the line, bombed his aerodromes, besides carrying out attacks on places of importance far behind the lines. It would seem probable that this has had the effect so far on the enemy of compelling him to keep back or to detail portions of his forces in the air for defensive purposes... the sound policy, then, which should guide all warfare in the air would seem to be this: to exploit the moral effect of the aeroplane on the enemy, but not let him exploit it on ourselves. Now this can only be done by attacking and by continuing to attack.'

Then, as has already been noted in Chapter 1, Field Marshal Smuts prophesised the day when strategic air bombardment would dominate warfare.

We can now see that the hopes and fears of the early theorists far exceeded the capabilities of the aircraft then available. Moreover, the full impact of strategic air bombardment, which was achieved at the end of World War 2, had been dramatically postponed by the contribution of ground-located radio early warning coupled with the construction of monoplane, high-performance fighters and, subsequently, airborne radar. The Luftwaffe over Southeast England, the RAF over Berlin and the USAF over Schweinfurt suffered heavy losses as air defences applied the technology and tactics devised by Watson-Watt, Bader and Kammhuber.

In 1967 the offensive power of the Israeli Air Force laid bare the Arab ground forces as comprehensively as the Luftwaffe in June 1941 had prepared the way for the blitzkreig in Western Russia, but only six years later the greatly increased ground-to-air, electronic and air-to-air defensive measures taken by the Arab forces in the Yom Kippur War made the offensive task of the Israeli Air Force much more complex. Ten years later still, that same air force had regained the upper hand in the defensive-offensive struggle – partly as a result of technological superiority, partly by superior tactics, partly by superior airmanship and partly by superior organisation, leadership and morale.

The offensive roles of British air power in the 1980s would, in the event of a failure of the basic deterrence posture, need to be discharged in a European environment

Below:
A Vulcan of No 50 Squadron carrying Shrike anti-radiation missiles of the kind used against Argentine radars in the Falklands. *Crown copyright photo by Flt Lt Mike Jenvey*

not unlike that of the Bekaa Valley, faced by the Israeli Air Force in 1983. In Europe however, Warsaw Pact air defences are not limited to one small region, but stretch back like a protective umbrella from the mobile ZSU-23 guns and SAMs deployed forward with the armoured divisions to the static high and low altitude SAMs integrated with the new generation of fighter and airborne early warning aircraft deployed in Eastern Europe and Western Russia, described in detail in Chapter 2. In fact Soviet air defences are so extensive that some critics of Western air power have suggested that the allocation of resources to offensive operations is a waste of valuable technology, manpower and effort. Yet the implications of such an abdication of offensive capability would have an impact on the British deterrent posture quite different from that envisaged by the critics, as even the most cursory examination of the opposing forces and their strategies illustrates.

As explained in the earlier analysis of Warsaw Pact strategy, Soviet forces in the European theatre have been considerably strengthened during the last decade. If they were to implement their avowed doctrine, they would rely on a surprise attack exploited by fast-moving ground forces which could be supported by both echeloned reinforcements and parallel thrusts to disperse and confuse Western defences. The whole would take place under favourable conditions of air superiority gained by neutralising NATO airfields, radar stations and control centres, by winning the local air battle and by protecting the Pact's own air-related assets. In all foreseeable circumstances the Warsaw Pact would have the initiative in choosing the timing, the location and the method of any attack on the West. NATO could still expect some warning time even if an attack should be made under cover of an exercise, but the irreversible facts of European geography, in the shape of the East European land mass, would seriously inhibit a Western defensive response in the breadth, depth and momentum sufficient to check a large scale Warsaw Pact offensive, no matter how effective NATO's rapid reinforcement in a period of tension or in the first hours of conflict.

At present however, a Warsaw Pact commander knows that immediately after he has launched his offensive he can expect a riposte from the allied air forces. He hopes to be able to co-ordinate his close air support, his longer range air attacks and his offensive on the ground. He would wish to accelerate or divert his reinforcing troops and supplies as circumstances dictate. Above all he would wish to sustain the momentum of his advance into Western Europe before any decision were made by NATO political leaders to invoke the power of nuclear weapons – assuming of course that the Warsaw Pact offensive had itself been limited to conventional weapons in the first place. He would like to do all that, but for the foreseeable future he is aware that because of the offensive strength of the NATO air forces, he cannot guarantee it. Conversely therefore, if ever the allied air forces should come to believe that their offensive role had become impossible to discharge, the potential enemy *could* plan to reinforce, resupply, repair, rest and recuperate without fear of disruption, denial or destruction. With how much more confidence could Warsaw Pact commanders predict the outcome of military adventures should their political masters be so inclined? Offensive air operations may, under some circumstances, be expensive in resource allocation. Their costs however become insignificant when compared with the possible costs to the West of a Warsaw Pact offensive which was launched and sustained from a sanctuary beyond artillery range across the Inner German Border.

But, quite apart from the strategic necessity of maintaining an offensive capability, it is easy to exaggerate the

Tornado GR1

Over 800 of Panavia's Multi-Role Combat Aircraft the Tornado have been ordered by the British, German and Italian Air Forces and the German Navy. Of these, 220 are interdictor-strike GR1s for the RAF, which will increase its operational capability to mount high speed, low level precision strikes in any weather.

Left:
Literally, at the sharp end: a Tornado GR1 at Honington.

Below:
It may be the blunt end, but the RB199 engines won't be far behind the rest of the aircraft! A close-up of the re-heat nozzles.

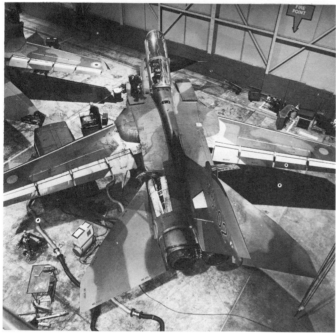

effective reality of enemy air defences as well as to underestimate the impact of modern Western defence suppression technology. It is for example highly unlikely that the Warsaw Pact air defences have satisfactorily resolved all the problems arising in an air space cluttered with surface-to-air defences, inhabited by friendly offensive and defensive aircraft and likely to be enshrouded by dense electronic activity. Indeed, evidence in the open press of Soviet air defence efficiency suggests that NATO air forces' task might not always be quite so formidable as worst case planning would suggest. In 1960, according to

Oleg Penkovsky, 13 SAM missiles were launched at Gary Powers' U-2 aircraft: 11 missed, one destroyed a MiG which was trying to catch him, and only the 13th brought him down. The tragic saga of the Korean airliner in 1983 was also noticeable for a lack of the kind of co-ordination familiar in Western air defence systems. The Western air forces, and the Royal Air Force in particular, are increasingly equipped to exploit enemy weaknesses as well as to capitalise on the inherent advantage of a weapon platform approaching close to the speed of sound, at heights where contours and ground clutter give natural protection against both ground and airborne radar defences and, in the closing stages, from any point in the compass.

The Vulcan Valedictory
While the 1980s sees the arrival of the Tornado, the maintained offensive contribution of the Jaguar and the proven combat effectiveness of the Harrier, it is also the decade which marks the withdrawal from service of the Avro/Hawker Siddeley Vulcan B2. For almost 30 years the

Vulcan first sustained the national nuclear deterrent and then after 1968 made a major contribution to SACEUR's theatre nuclear capability, while retaining a potential for speedy modification to carry 21,000lb of conventional weapons.

In 1981, with the imminent arrival of Tornado into squadron service, the Vulcan force began to be disbanded. Many of the squadrons' air and ground crews began to cross train to the new multi-role successor. First to disband was No 230 OCU at RAF Scampton, there being no further need to provide manpower for the operational squadrons. Next went the Scampton wing: Nos 617, 35 and 27 Squadrons. On 29 April 1982 the first of the Waddington wing, No 9 Squadron, disbanded prior to being re-formed at RAF Honington as the first Tornado squadron. Thereupon the plans to disband the remaining Waddington squadrons – Nos 44, 50 and 101 – were abruptly changed as a result of events in the South Atlantic.

Air plans and options presented by the RAF staffs to the government after the outbreak of hostilities over the Falklands still remain classified, but it is possible to speculate reasonably confidently about probable salient points in the strategic assessment. Stanley airfield could, given a certain amount of Argentinian ingenuity, provide forward operating base facilities for Mirage and Skyhawk aircraft. Once there, their threat to any British task force or air activity was self-evident. It was therefore highly desirable for the single main runway to be so damaged as to render it unusable for any high-performance jet aircraft.

On the other hand even to reach Stanley airfield would be a major undertaking for the RAF, quite apart from having to inflict serious damage upon it. The Falkland Islands were 3,900 miles from the nearest RAF staging post on Ascension Island which in turn was 4,100 miles distance from the home base at Waddington. The Vulcan's unrefuelled range, depending upon the usual variables of height, speed and weight, was in the order of 3–3,500 miles.

The decision was taken quickly: a small number of Vulcans was converted to carry a full 21,000lb conventional bomb load and fitted with Carousel inertial navigation systems transferred swiftly from a batch of ex-British Airways Super VC10s already purchased by the MoD. In-flight refuelling equipment, not used by the Vulcan force for some 15 years, was speedily refurbished and air-to-air refuelling training instituted with the Victor crews of Nos 55 and 57 Squadrons from Marham. Westinghouse AN/ALQ-101 ECM pods of the type carried by No 208 Buccaneer Squadron were fitted for additional protection against the Argentinian Boeing 707 believed to be operating in the theatre as an airborne early warning aircraft. The Argentinian forces had occupied the Falklands on 2 April: on 9 April the ground crews and air crews at Waddington and Marham began their preparations; on 29 April the first two Vulcans prepared to take part in Operation 'Black Buck' landed safely at Wideawake Airfield, Ascension Island. Two days later the first attack was launched on Stanley airfield.

After the Napoleonic Wars, the German strategist

Clausewitz reflected on what he called 'The Fog of War', and the 'friction' of unexpected events which, like sand in a machine, can upset even the best laid plans. On this occasion however the quality of RAF planning, operational skill and cool bravery saw the plans home. Shortly after take-off on 1 May, the first Vulcan went unserviceable and had to return to Wideawake. The airborne reserve aircraft crewed by Flt Lts Martin Withers, Bob Wright, Gordon Graham, Hugh Prior and Richard Russell, with Flg Off Peter Taylor as co-pilot, took over the mission, passed down the Victor in-flight refuelling chain, and accurately bombed the centre of Stanley airfield, placing the first bomb in the middle of the main runway. If Argentinian eye-witness accounts do become available they should make interesting reading, because the success of the attack lay not just in the achievement of the aim of putting the runway beyond fast jet use, but in placing the entire garrison under threat of air attack. There was to be no sanctuary on the islands and indeed there now had to be question marks over the sanctuary of the airfields on the South American mainland. It is most unlikely that political authority would have been granted for a Vulcan attack on one of the mainland bases; indeed there were scant Vulcan or Victor resources to mount such an attack even had a political directive been received. But at the time the government in Buenos Aires could neither forecast the extent of the British government's reaction to the invasion nor estimate reliably the capability of the long range Vulcan-Victor team. Doubts were reinforced by four more sorties flown against the Islands: two more against the airfield and its installations, and two against radars which had been marking the position of the Task Force as well as providing early warning of air attacks. The first Shrike

attack put the search radar out for 12 hours, but apparently the Argentinians had noted the lessons of the 1973 Middle East war and switched off as the second Vulcan came within range. After attacking the airfield radars this aircraft had a tense return journey after its in-flight refuelling probe tip snapped off at the outset of its Victor contact. It made a widely publicised emergency diversion to Rio de Janeiro with a Shrike missile still hung up on one pylon, thereby giving rise to the blandly uncorrected report that it had been carrying AIM-9L Sidewinders.

Thus after 28 years of preparedness – 28 years of training for a role which thankfully was never demanded of it – the Vulcan and its crews saw combat of a completely different kind, in a different hemisphere, after less than 28 days pre-employment training. First flown on 30 August 1952, the Vulcan had entered service with No 230 OCU in August 1956. It had carried free-fall nuclear and conventional weapons, had been modified to work as a strategic reconnaissance aircraft, and now it ended its days as a bomber in the airfield interdiction and defence suppression role. Indeed, had the war not ended when it did, it might actually have been fitted with Sidewinders, whereupon no doubt the Vulcan crews would have received some old fashioned looks from their more traditional fighter pilot colleagues.

Below:
Terrain following by Tornados of No 9 Squadron from Honington. *BAe*

Right:
Pre-flight Tornado systems check on a No 9 Squadron aircraft.

the triplex electrical flying controls and automatic stabilisation. The Command and Stability Augmentation System (CSAS) automatically compensates for configuration changes during flight and several pilot reports have testified to the aircraft's high stability in turbulent air conditions. Maximum speed is in excess of Mach 2 in level flight.

Navigation to the target is also highly automated. The auto-pilot can follow a flight plan automatically or it can be updated by the navigator in the back seat as he monitors a combined map and radar and TV displays, and makes radar or laser position fixes. The terrain-following radar is considerably more advanced than that on the F-111 and can, by integration with the CSAS, guide the aircraft at high speed at a predetermined height above the ground. Thus maximum advantage may be taken of contours to evade detection by enemy radar.

Tornado can lift up to 16,000lb of weapons, rather more than the regular Lancaster bombload, on three under-fuselage and four underwing pylons. But, more importantly, it can deliver them with much greater accuracy. Automatic computerised radar target identification can be monitored by a head-up display and followed by automatic procedures to weapon release point. The final precision is achieved by laser rangefinder but at any time the pilot may modify the attack profile or select a completely new target.

The combination of these qualities in Tornado has produced an aircraft which can deliver a large conventional or nuclear weapon load with great accuracy in all weathers by day or by night. In any future conflict an enemy cannot be expected to cease fire at dusk or in bad weather and Tornado's 24-hour availability will be indispensable to NATO. Its very low level, high-speed penetration, 800kt at 200ft, together with automatic radar warning and jamming equipment, a chaff dispenser and countermeasures to infra-red missiles, will reduce its vulnerability and thereby increase its availability and effectiveness. Its potential recalls that of the World War 2 Mosquito whose relative invulnerability greatly increased its cost-effectiveness also. Finally, Tornado's ability to operate from damaged runways and other surfaces will reduce its vulnerability on the ground.

As it was, the five crews specially selected for the missions returned to their squadrons, and the sad process of disbandment continued: No 101 Squadron in August 1982, No 44 Squadron in December. Six aircraft however remained in service with No 50 Squadron until 1984, in yet another role which forms part of the story narrated in Chapter 5. Meanwhile, the major offensive roles of British air power were inherited by the most formidable weapon system yet to be flown by the RAF: the Panavia Tornado.

Tornado

Tornado is the product of allied collaboration by the British Aerospace corporation, Messerschmitt-Boelkow-Blohm and Aer Italia. It is powered by twin Turbo-Union RB199s which have the highest thrust-to-volume ratio of any turbine engine in the world. They also have a low specific fuel consumption but for short take-off and combat manoeuvres a high reheat thrust is available. Yet, with the aid of thrust reversal, Tornado can be landed on less than 500yd of runway, an extremely important operational consideration for future European conflict. Both attack (GR1) and interceptor (F2) versions have variable sweep wings, but those on the GR1 are swept manually back to 67°, whereas the F2 has autosweep. Consequently, at high speed and low altitudes high wing loading is possible giving a very smooth ride at Mach 0.9 at 200ft which reduces crew fatigue and enhances instrument monitoring, thereby greatly improving the overall effectiveness of the weapon platform. Handling benefits from

Training for Tornado

RAF aircrew destined for one of the Tornado squadrons first meet their new aircraft at RAF Cottesmore, in the Rutland region of Cambridgeshire. There they join the Tri-National Tornado Training Establishment (TTTE), which received its first aircraft in July 1980 and which was opened formally in January 1981. The TTTE trains pilots and navigators for the Royal Air Force, German Air Force, German Navy and the Italian Air Force who will fly the interdictor/strike version of the aircraft. Of the 50 Tornados on the unit, 22 are German, 21 are British and seven are Italian. The Tornado Operational Conversion Unit has three squadrons plus a standards squadron along with an engineering wing and an administration wing. Flying instructors are drawn from all three nations, while the majority of the ground crews are British, since aircraft servicing and the provision of most of the support services are the responsibility of the UK. The 13-week conversion course comprises four weeks ground school and nine weeks flying training to a syllabus and standard

agreed by the three
countries. Because of this it is possible
for a Royal Air Force student to be taught by a German
instructor in Italian aircraft, thereby increasing interoperability between the three nations' front line Tornado
squadrons and enhancing NATO's overall operational
effectiveness. On successful completion of the course the
air crews move on to their national units for tactics and
weapons training.

Royal Air Force crews move across East Anglia to the
Tornado Weapons Conversion Unit (TWCU), formed at
RAF Honington in July 1981. In May 1982 at the Hanover
Air Show, the then Commanding Officer of TWCU, Wg
Cdr Duncan Griffiths, graphically described the range
and effectiveness of Tornado operations.

'We practised all the bombing modes of Tornado including
the low level lay-down, which is a high-speed low level
attack, the conventional type of attack using a shallow
dive with visually aimed weapons through the Head Up
Display, and the Loft Attack which is a stand-off delivery
from pulling up some four miles away from the target . . .

'We have done some trials work already in preparation for the operational squadrons to try and evaluate the best way of actually using the aeroplane, using its navigation and weapon aiming facilities against real targets. There are two phases we have looked at so far. The first was the visual phase: this is not Tornado's bread and butter stuff of course, but bearing in mind that it does get to be daylight for almost half the time, we might have to use this form of delivery. By using a completely silent attack, that is to say not using any of the radars in the aeroplane at all, we have been able to use the facilities on the aeroplane to ensure that we get to a "no show" target over a difficult range. A range in fact where in the past people have only

Above:
Returning to base: Tornado GR1 from No XV Squadron at Laarbruch.

Right:
Pre-flight checks in a Tornado back seat.

guaranteed the first run attack if the target has been marked with a laser marker, and we have had an almost 100% success in acquiring and hitting the targets. This again is a very commendable thing to be able to say at this stage of development. On the radar side – the second phase of our trial was concerned with radar-attacking targets over land – we found again that the radar has got a performance that is unparalleled. We are having to rethink our radar tracking techniques. The radar is so good that what should be a big prominent radar target is really no longer any use; you need to look for really small pin-point positions, and the radar can do this. During this trial we found that they had laid a telephone cable in front of the target area. They dug a little trench, perhaps no more than 2ft deep, put a wire in it, covered it up again and it was a little ridge about 2in high, and that painted a clear line on the radar. This gives you an idea of the sort of performance that you can get from this radar. So I think that we should have no problems being able to utilise the full weapon capability in bad weather using radar.'

The Tornado Squadrons

Two weeks later, the first Royal Air Force Tornado interdictor strike squadron formed at RAF Honington. No 9 was the first RFC Squadron to be equipped with radio in 1914 and since then, with the exception of a few months at the end of World War 1, has remained a bomber squadron. It took part in the raid against the experimental rocket station at Peenemunde and with No 617 Squadron its Lancasters attacked and sank the German battleship *Tirpitz* at Tromso in 1944. Flt Sgt George Thompson, a wireless operator with No 9 Squadron, on a daylight raid in January 1945, earned one of Bomber Command's 23 Victoria Crosses whilst saving the lives of two fellow crew members in his burning aircraft. Later, in 1956, the Squadron's Canberras took part in the Suez operation. It has now returned to the base from where in 1939 it flew Mk 1 Wellingtons. However, instead of having its aircraft displaced across the airfield, they are all hidden away in the first hardened aircraft shelters (HAS) to be built for the Royal Air Force in the UK. Also protected are

the Squadron Planning and Operations areas, a dormitory for 45 people, cooking facilities, stores of fresh uncontaminated water and facilities for chemical decontamination. While the Tornado itself has brought new challenges to the aircrew, so operating from hardened shelters has encouraged devolution of responsibility across a larger number of junior NCOs who no longer work under the eagle eye of one senior NCO along a single flight line. As Wg Cdr Peter Gooding, the Squadron Commander, observed during a briefing in October 1982: 'We can quite comfortably operate, and I mean operate as opposed to store, two aircraft in each shelter. In all that we do, our aim is to operate in peace as near as we can to the way we would do so in war.'

An example of that wartime potential was demonstrated in November 1982 when a Tornado of No 9 Squadron, piloted by Flt Lt Ian Dugmore with Sqn Ldr Mike Holmes as his navigator, carried out a simulated attack on Akrotiri airfield in Cyprus. During the 4,300-mile return flight from Honington the Tornado was refuelled a number of times by Victors of Nos 55 and 57 Squadrons at medium altitude and by a Buccaneer from No 237 OCU Honington at low level. The Tornado carried a representative weapons

Tornado JP233 Weapon Trials

It has long been recognised that one of the most effective counter-air operations is to prevent the enemy from using his airfields. With this in mind Hunting Engineering Ltd has designed the JP233 anti-airfield weapon, two of which can be carried by the Tornado GR1.

Left:
The modern equivalent of the bomb trolley.

Below left:
Lifting the weapons to the fuselage.

Below:
The armed Tornado ready to leave the HAS.

load for the 12-hour flight which included a tactical low-level phase of some 600 miles.

Six weeks later the second Tornado squadron was formed at Marham and also assumed a famous number plate: 617. This squadron was formed at Scampton in March 1943 with the express purpose of attacking the Ede, Mohne and Sorpe dams in the heart of the German industrial Ruhr. After the legendary successful raid of 16 May it remained in service as a specialist low-level unit as well as contributing to main bombing and pathfinding duties in No 5 Group, including raids with 12,000lb and 22,000lb bombs on V-weapon bases and on the *Tirpitz*. It was only the second RAF squadron to produce two VCs: Wg Cdr Guy Gibson for the dams raid and Wg Cdr Leonard Cheshire for his consistent leadership on every mission no matter how hazardous or difficult, and for pioneering very low level target marking. The Squadron flew Vulcans at Scampton from 1968 until its temporary disbandment in 1981. Like No 9 Squadron, No 617 Squadron's wartime role would be to conduct strike/attack operations in the European theatre and peacetime training is geared to this mission.

Across the airfield are the hardened shelters of No 27 Squadron, the third squadron to re-equip with Tornado after a short disbandment at Scampton. No 27 Squadron inherited the RAF's strategic reconnaissance role from the Victors of No 543 Squadron in 1974. No 27 has returned to the 'family' after a varied existence since its formation in 1915 during which it has discharged reconnaissance, bombing, imperial policing, training, fighter, anti-shipping, ground attack (when its Commanding Officer, Wg Cdr J. B. Nicholson won the VC) and jungle rescue roles, transport during the Berlin airlift, the attack at Suez, and Blue Steel responsibilities during the period of the deterrent force.

Meanwhile, Tornado re-equipment also began across the Channel in Royal Air Force Germany. Since 1972 RAF Laarbruch had been the home of RAFG's longer range offensive squadrons equipped with Buccaneer S Mk 2s tasked with 'deeper interdiction', or missions similar to those flown by the Jaguar but further behind the battlefield region against large concentrations, supply

areas, headquarters and similar targets whose destruction would have a major impact on the battle itself. During 1983 and 1984 Nos XV and 16 Squadrons at Laarbruch began to convert to Tornado.

On 1 September the first Tornado sortie by No XV Squadron was navigated by Wg Cdr Barry Dove, the new Squadron Commander; two months later the Squadron standard was formally handed over from the Buccaneer element at a formal parade taken by Air Marshal Sir Patrick Hine, Commander-in-Chief RAF Germany and Commander Second Allied Tactical Air Force. In his address he not only reminded his audience of the long traditions of No XV Squadron, he explained why as an allied air commander he was so pleased to see the advent of Tornado in RAFG.

'Our German friends may not know that a Standard is awarded by the Sovereign to those RAF squadrons that have completed at least 25 years service. No XV Squadron's Standard was awarded in 1952, collected in 1956 and formally presented in 1961 by Her Royal Highness the Duchess of Kent. The Squadron has come a very long way since it became operational in BE2 biplanes in France in 1915, and eight of its battle honours from two World Wars are inscribed either side of the Squadron badge on the Standard before us. But the Squadron motto "Aim Sure" has never been more apt than today with re-equipment to the Tornado now taking place.

'However, as C-in-C RAF Germany and COMT-WOATAF, I am able to view the changeover to Tornado with greater detachment. And I see it marking a great step forward in terms of our operational capability to penetrate

Below:
A Tornado GR1 releasing the runway break-up and area denial weapons during test flights.

Bottom:
The spent JP233 weapon casing displayed after sub-munition delivery. *All Hunting Engineering Ltd*

enemy defences at high speed and very low-level, by day or night and in virtually any weather, and then to attack key targets blind with great accuracy. With new weapons also entering the inventory over the next few years, we shall be able – if deterrence should ever fail, which God forbid – to neutralise enemy airfields for hours, perhaps days, at a time, thereby helping NATO air forces in a major way to gain the air initiative without which forward defence of the Federal Republic in war would be impossible.

'It is a source of particular pleasure to me that RAF Germany will be building up its Tornado force in parallel with a similar deployment by the Luftwaffe. For that symbolises not only the very close co-operation between our two countries together with Italy, in producing this magnificent aircraft, but also the metamorphosis that has taken place in the relationships between the two air forces since their aerial battles during the Second World War. The respect that we held for each other then as contestants has given way to a bond of Anglo–Saxon comradeship that has never been closer. Long may it remain so.'

No 16 Squadron also has an illustrious history. Formed at St Omer in 1915, hence its nickname 'The Saints', it was mainly occupied in tactical reconnaissance, artillery observation and photography missions in World War 1. Between the wars it specialised in Army co-operation roles and took its Lysanders to France in 1940. Later re-equipping with Mustangs, Tomahawks and Tempests it discharged a variety of fighter-bomber duties until the end of the war. In 1958 it began to fly interdictor Canberra B8s at Laarbruch, re-equipped with Buccaneer S2s in 1972, and now has become the second Tornado squadron in RAFG.

Future Tornado Developments

Deployment of Tornado squadrons will continue steadily until the RAF's re-equipment programme is complete later in this decade. The Bruggen Jaguar wing will convert and then No 2 (PR) Squadron at Laarbruch. Meanwhile, the operational effectiveness of the aircraft will be continuously improved by mid-term updates and the entry into service of new weapon systems. The aircraft's own effectiveness is being progressively uprated by the installation of the more powerful Mk 10K version of the RB199 engine and by the extension of the afterburner.

Already in 1983, aircraft at No XV Squadron could be observed at RAF Laarbruch carrying Sky Shadow elec-

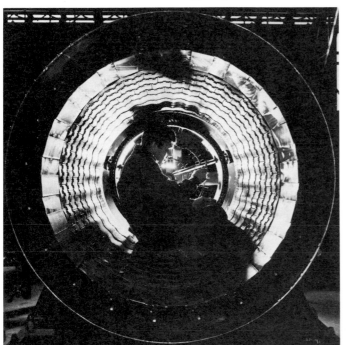

Jaguar

Although planned for replacement in RAF Germany by the Tornado GR1, the Anglo-French Jaguar is still a potent strike aircraft. It can deliver a wide range of weapons, including nuclear bombs, and is able to operate from autobahns if its home runway is damaged.

Left:
Engine repair at Bruggen. *Crown copyright photo by Sgt Don Lambert*

Below:
A Jaguar T2 shares the backyard of its Bruggen HAS with a visiting Tornado from No 617 Squadron. *Crown copyright photo by Sgt Don Lambert*

tronic countermeasures pods and Sidewinder AA missiles as well as an offensive load of freefall or laser-guided bombs. In the immediate future however, Tornado will carry the JP233 anti-airfield weapon designed by Hunting Engineering Ltd. The rationale underlying JP233 was explained in 1982 by the then AVM David Harcourt-Smith when he was Assistant Chief of the Air Staff for Operational Requirements.

'The classic illustration of offensive counter-air action is undoubtedly the virtual destruction on the ground of the Arab air forces during the 1967 war with Israel. Since then, however, it has become increasingly difficult to achieve success because most combat aircraft are now dispersed and protected in hardened aircraft shelters. Our studies have shown that difficulties of target acquisition, particularly in bad weather or at night, and weapon-to-target matching considerations indicate that the most lucrative targets on airfields are operating surfaces.

'Currently we plan to attack airfield operating surfaces with a range of general purpose weapons employing a variety of delivery profiles. However, it has been recognised for some time that there is an urgent requirement for a weapon specifically designed for this task if airfields are to be closed for a significant period of time. It was with this in mind that the Air Staff Requirement for JP233, the Airfield Attack Weapon, was raised. This requirement calls for a weapon which will crater operating surfaces and support areas and simultaneously distribute a large number of area denial sub-munitions to prevent the timely repair of the craters. This weapon can be used in many ways, but the design has been matched to the weapon system delivery accuracy of Tornado operating at low level in blind, jammed conditions. JP233 will enter service later in this decade and will provide an airfield attack capability second to none.'

In February 1984 *Military Technology* published a full description of JP233.

'Although belonging to the same category of fixed dispensers as MW-1, the British JP233 (currently under development by Hunting Engineering) differs from the German system in that it was specifically designed for the counter-air role. It is however also possible to use it for attacking area targets such as massed vehicles, railway yards, road networks, and so on . . .'

'In its standard version, configured for the TORNADO GR1, the JP233 is a large ventral pod (length 4.025m, width 1.140m, loaded weight 2,335kg) subdivided into two sections: the front element houses 215 HB876 area denial

Above left:
Sooty's at work at the coalface at Bruggen. *Crown copyright photo by Sgt Don Lambert*

Left:
'Golf Juliet' of No 54 Squadron on a low pass across Coltishall airfield.

Right:
'Golf Kilo' of No 54 Squadron returns to base trailing its base shute.

mines, and the aft one carries 30 SG357 runway cratering bomblets. Both types of sub-munitions are scattered simultaneously and in a co-ordinated sequence.

'The SG357s are carried nose uppermost, and are ejected rearward at an angle of 30 degrees bursting through a light metal panel which forms the bottom of the dispenser. Ejection is by rams operated by gas cartridges.

'The HB876s are ejected outwards by tubes angled at different values (from 15 to 35 degrees) in order to maximise dispersion. Each tube contains one, two or three mines according to its position.

'The SG357 is a dual-effect runway cratering munition very akin to the STABO: it descends to the ground with a small parachute, and a distance sensor triggers the detonation of a shaped charge which pierces a hole through the concrete runway. The second HE warhead passes through the hole, and it is detonated under the runway by a time fuze.

'The HB876 can act as a mine proper, and as a retarded effect bomblet with a delay of up to some hours. The HB876s slow down considerably repair activities.'

Tornado will carry two JP233 weapons in addition to its defensive equipment and it is possible to speculate on the implications of its attacks on Warsaw Pact air operations. It is probable that the Pact would attempt to mount carefully co-ordinated attacks on Western targets to achieve the maximum concentration of force in a given time in a given area, or, conversely, to exploit an attack by carefully planned secondary waves. Consequently, while a Tornado attack could close an airfield for several hours, the disruption of the enemy air offensive achieved by shorter closure could be equally dramatic. Moreover, even the awareness that airfields could be subject to interdiction might be sufficient to induce caution in a commander whose success may hinge upon smoothly co-ordinated operations.

Tornado's ability to pierce even the most sophisticated hostile radar-assisted defence will be enhanced still further when it is equipped with the British Aerospace Dynamics ALARM missile later this decade, which is designed to meet a RAF air staff target for a weapon able to detect, home on and destroy enemy radar. Early information released on the weapon indicated that it had a parachute retarded 'loiter' capability as well as the traditional mode of direct attack on the threat radar emitter, while it could be quickly reprogrammed to respond to a variety of defensive systems.

Meanwhile, further generations of weapons are being studied by the RAF. The modified BL755 cluster bomb, able to penetrate thicker armour over a wider area than its predecessor, is likely to remain in service until the end of the decade, but thereafter it is highly probable that conventional weapon technology will offer a range of weapons which an aircraft could deliver from beyond the range of point surface-to-air defences. They could include powered or unpowered missiles equipped with sub-munition anti-armour warheads, which could either themselves be homing or be dispersible as minelets. As engine technology and guidance systems become proportionately smaller so conventionally-armed cruise missiles with self-homing munitions using infra-red or millimetric wave radar become an increasingly practical proposition. Together they suggest that in aerial warfare the pendulum may be swinging back again towards the offensive.

The Jaguar Force

The next aircraft in the RAF inventory to be replaced by the Tornado GR1s will be the Jaguars in RAF Germany at Bruggen but the close air support provided from the UK by the Coltishall wing is likely to remain Jaguar-delivered for several years yet.

Unlike the squadrons in RAF Germany, however, the Jaguar units at Coltishall would not necessarily operate in the Central Region of Europe. They are assigned to SACEUR's Strategic Reserve (Air) which is a force of RAF and USAF squadrons normally based in the UK, which could redeploy at short notice to airfields anywhere on the

Harrier

What can be said about Harrier that has not already been said
by the aircraft's own performance? Quite simply, Harrier is
unique, and no-one can be in any doubt as to its ability to
achieve its operational tasks in time of war.

Above:
A GR3 of No 1 Squadron in Arctic camouflage; crews training
in 1981 had no idea how valuable that training would be later in
the South Atlantic.

Below:
Harrier T4 of No 4 Squadron on exercise in RAFG. *BAe*

mainland of Europe to strengthen defences or to reinforce air attacks on enemy armour and airfields. Consequently, also unlike their colleagues in Germany, these crews are trained in air-to-air refuelling. One of the Jaguar squadrons has an alternative operational role as part of the air element of the UK Mobile Force, a self-supporting air and land force equipped to counter armour and mechanised infantry and trained for operations in each area of Allied Command Europe. A further mobile force, with a more restricted strategic role, is the Allied Command Europe Mobile Force (AMF) which is a multi-national land and air force which could rapidly deploy to either the northern or southern flanks of the Alliance. Its function is primarily to demonstrate promptly the collective resolve of the Alliance rather than to provide extensive defence in depth.

The Jaguar pilot workload is demanding and it is no coincidence that Nos 6 and 54 Squadrons have long and proud traditions. No 6 has been associated with close air support for the greater part of its history since forming at Farnborough in January 1914. From 1919 to 1969 it saw unbroken service in the Middle East, quelling insurgency in Iraq, peacekeeping in Palestine, and mounting ground attack sweeps in the Western Desert against the Italians and Rommel's Afrika Korps. Subsequently, the Squadron flew Spitfires, Venoms and Canberras until 1969 when it disbanded for the first time in 55 years. Later that year it re-formed in the UK at Coningsby with Phantoms in the ground attack and tactical reconnaissance roles before converting to the Jaguar GR1 in 1974.

No 54 Squadron, on the other hand, has a long tradition as a fighter squadron since its formation at Castle Bromwich in World War 1. During World War 2 it was heavily involved in the Battle of Britain, flying Spitfires from Hornchurch. Among its distinguished pilots were Plt Off C. F. Gray who shot down 16 enemy aircraft, Flg Off D. A. P. McMullen who shot down 13, and Flt Lt (later Air Commodore) Al Deere. After 1945 it was successively equipped with Vampires, Meteors and Hunters until in March 1960 it received Hunter FGA9s and began to specialise in ground attack operations. It also received Jaguar GR1s in 1974.

The first Jaguar GR1 deployed to Bruggen in 1975 and there are now four squadrons in the wing: Nos 14, 17, 20 and 31 Squadrons. If the Warsaw Pact ground forces should ever cross the Inner German Border, the Bruggen wing would be swiftly and heavily engaged, and to operate effectively the Jaguar crews train to fly down to 250ft at 500kt and, if necessary, both lower and faster. The Jaguar's small size makes it a difficult target and its twin Adour engines leave no tell-tale smoke plumes. It is armed with 30mm Aden guns and can deliver cluster weapons, free-fall 500lb or 1,000lb bombs, laser-guided bombs or, should their use be authorised by the political leaders of NATO, nuclear weapons. Its navigational and weapon aiming sub-system (NAVWASS) incorporates a head-up-display projected on the canopy in front of the pilot and may be pre-programmed with wind speeds at height, way points, initial point prior to making the attack run, target position and much more information which, in previous generations, would have taxed a navigator and bomb-aimer to the full. Moreover, the NAVWASS has been greatly improved since its first installation and the black boxes on which it depends are steadily being reduced in size. The laser ranger and marked-target seeker may be used in conjunction with a forward air controller equipped with a laser target marker. When the aircraft approaches the target it is illuminated by the laser beam of the target marker. The marked target seeker in the aircraft automatically acquires and tracks the laser energy reflected from the target, driving the pilot's head-up display to indicate target position in elevation and azimuth. The distance to the target is then measured automatically and, even if the target is not being illuminated, the airborne equipment may still be used as a range-finder. Consequently, the pilot's search task is reduced and he may not actually need to see his target at all. The aircraft demands great precision from its crews, not simply because of the need for navigation and bombing accuracy, but because many missions could comprise eight or more aircraft, and timing over the target must be exact to the second to reduce the efficiency of the defences, increase the impact of the raid and, indeed, to reduce the chances of air-to-air accidents. Not surprisingly therefore, competition between the four Jaguar squadrons at Bruggen is extremely keen and standards high. No 14, located in Germany since 1946, was the first to operate the new aircraft in April 1975. No 14 has spent most of its RAF service overseas either in the Middle East or in Germany and during World War 1 had a detachment of aircraft working with the guerilla forces of Lawrence of Arabia. No 17 Squadron, which also began to re-equip with Jaguars in 1975, has a long history of fighter-ground attack which includes a famous sortie in World War 1 by the then Second Lieutenant John Slessor against 200 mounted Turkish troops. No 20 Squadron, which took its Jaguars in 1977, has served almost entirely overseas since its formation in 1915 and, from 1932, mainly in the offensive support role. No 31 Squadron, on the other hand, discharged a variety of tasks between its formation at Farnborough in 1915 and its conversion to Jaguars at Bruggen in 1976, including transport and photographic reconnaissance. In June 1980 it was demonstrated that previous variety was no bar to current effectiveness when Flt Lt Ian Kenyon won the Broadhurst Trophy for low-level shallow angle bombing and achieved the best individual score for visual lay-down bombing in the biennial Tactical Air Meet held at the USAF's Ramstein AFB, competing against other highly professional crews from Belgium, Canada, West Germany, Norway, the United States and France. After 12 tactical missions in the Air Meet the national units were separated and, after drawing lots, re-formed with international teams for the two competitive missions designed to test weapons delivery, navigation and tactical reconnaissance. Competitions may also include an operational turn-round to give the ground crews an opportunity to demonstrate the skills without which the best pilot in the world could achieve nothing. Dispersal of aircraft to HAS has, of course, put an additional premium on the teamwork needed to refuel, rearm and service an aircraft in the shortest possible time.

Such competition is one of the ways in which the Bruggen squadrons can demonstrate their constant high state of effectiveness which, as in the case of their interceptor colleagues, is the best way of reducing the likelihood that they will be tested in the war. Such a Meet is not solely or, indeed, primarily a competition. It is an opportunity for NATO crews to work together on various kinds of offensive sorties in a simulated hostile environ-

AFB in Nevada. They carried free-fall or laser-guided bombs, drop tanks, a chaff dispenser and an ECM pod to combat the dense array of simulated Warsaw Pact air defences which are a characteristic feature of 'Red Flag' exercises. Indeed, although the Bruggen Jaguars will ultimately be replaced by Tornados, 'their operational capability has been significantly enhanced', in the words of the station commander in 1984, Gp Capt John Thomson,' by the acquisition not only of the laser-guided bombs, chaff and ECM pods but also by flare dispensers designed to decoy heat seeking missiles.' Meanwhile, they continue to demonstrate their ability to maintain operations, even if Bruggen's runways were to be temporarily damaged, by recovering to autobahns and by using taxiways for both take-off and landing.

In common with all the other NATO squadrons deployed in AAFCE, they must face the rigours of TACEVAL: the no-notice simulation of a full wartime alert. The tactical evaluations serve four main purposes: to assess the ability of RAF units to meet their operational tasks, to ascertain if any deficiencies exist, to report to the Commander-in-Chief RAFG on the operational effective-

No 1 Squadron Heads South

Above left:
'. . . if anyone had told me . . . we would be fighting a war from an aircraft carrier some 8,000 miles from home, I frankly would not have believed them'. Wg Cdr Peter Squire leads No 1 Squadron on to HMS *Hermes.*   *SSgt C. J. Bowman*

Left:
Safely down and a warm welcome from the *Hermes* flight deck crew for Wg Cdr Squire.   *SSgt C. J. Bowman*

Right:
GR3s preparing for take-off from HMS *Hermes* during Operation 'Corporate'.   *SSgt C. J. Bowman*

Below:
GR3s, Sea Harriers and an RN Sea King on a cold and foggy *Hermes* flight deck during the Falklands war.

ment of 'enemy' aircraft, SAMs and electronic counter-measures, while supported by 'friendly' reconnaissance and electronic counter countermeasures and other kinds of defence suppression. Jaguar is, of course, equipped with integral hostile radar warning equipment.

However, the Bruggen crews do not have to wait for a biennial exercise to demonstrate their effectiveness. Because NATO is entirely a defensive Alliance and because in any conflict the Warsaw Pact could expect to have the advantage of choosing the time, place and method of the attack, it is highly likely that the Bruggen wing would first be fighting over West German territory to stop the invading forces. Consequently, the Jaguars can fly regularly over the roads and fields where they will be likely to operate until every contour becomes familiar to the crews. Longer sorties can be simulated by attacks on training ranges either in Western Europe, back in the UK or on the NATO range at Decimomannu in Sardinia. In addition, they participate in exercises in North America. In winter 1983 for example, nine Jaguars from the Bruggen wing participated in Exercise 'Red Flag 83–2' at Nellis

ness of his forces and to report to SACEUR on the status of RAF units which are assigned to Allied Command Europe. TACEVAL tests not only the preparedness and operational effectiveness of the aircrew, but the strength of the logistic and other supporting facilities and the ability of all elements of the unit to survive and operate in hostile air and ground conditions. As if the approximately annual TACEVAL was not enough, station commanders will order their own periodic evaluations which will demand standards at least as high as those set by the NATO teams. An extremely important by-product of the TACEVAL system has been to emphasise how essential it is for everyone on a station to work together as a war-fighting team. Indeed it is possible for a station to produce the best possible operational effectiveness results in TACEVAL and still receive a very critical unsatisfactory overall assessment if its supporting elements have been found wanting. Happily, RAFG stations have never had such an embarrassment. Indeed, they have consistently achieved the best evaluation standards of any units in the Central Region.

The Harrier Force

As the Tornado wings begin to deploy on the airfields west of the Rhine, an equally well known, but very different aircraft will continue to be located, some of the time, at RAF Gutersloh, well to the east and only 80 miles from the nearest section of the Inner German Border, the home of Nos 3 and 4 Harrier Squadrons and No 230 Squadron equipped with Puma helicopters. No 3 Squadron was actually formed before the Royal Flying Corps as it flew as No 2 (Aeroplane) Company of the Air Battalion of the Royal Engineers in 1911. During its renowned fighter and ground attack history it shot down 288 pilotless V-1 aircraft over England in the later stages of World War 2 prior to becoming part of Second Tactical Air Force. Thereafter, it has served in Germany, converting to Harriers at Wildenrath in 1971 and moving to Gutersloh in 1977 when Gutersloh and Wildenrath exchanged roles and aircraft. No 4 Squadron was formed in 1912, a few months after No 3, and has for most of its history distinguished itself in the fighter-ground attack and fighter reconnaissance roles. In August 1970 it became the

Above:
A GR3 armed with naval 2in rockets.

first squadron to operate fixedwing V/STOL jet fighters outside Britain when it re-equipped with the Harrier GR Mk 1 at Wildenrath. With No 3 Squadron it also moved to Gutersloh in 1977. By 1980, both squadrons were flying the GR Mk 3 and the two-seat T Mk 4.

Harrier is powered by a single Rolls-Royce Pegasus vectored thrust turbofan jet engine, which by means of two pairs of rotatable nozzles can vector the exhaust gases from 20% forward of the vertical to horizontally aft. This configuration allows the aircraft not only to land and to take off vertically, but by varying the vector in flight it can decelerate extremely rapidly and attain a very high degree of manoeuvrability. Such a combination makes the Harrier a difficult and dangerous target for fighters which theoretically have far superior performance. It has a maximum level flight speed of about Mach 0.95 and is supersonic in a shallow dive. It has a radius of action of 450 miles and its ferry or operational ranges may be extended by in-flight refuelling. It can carry 5,000lb of weapons on seven external points which could include SNEB rockets, Aden 30mm cannon in wing pods, free-fall or retarded bombs, but its usual weapon load is the 600lb BL755 cluster bomb which distributes a pattern of sub-munitions lethal to ground forces over a wide area.

It is, however, not its weapon load but its method of operation which makes the Harrier unique in European air power. In a period of rising tension, Wildenrath, Laarbruch and Bruggen would seem deserted, with their Phantoms, Tornados and Jaguars securely protected in their closed HAS. But Gutersloh might really be deserted, at least by the Harrier force which would literally have gone to ground, scattered among the woods, barns and even villages of the surrounding countryside close to the ground forces of No 1 (British) Corps of the Allied Northern Army Group with which Nos 3 and 4 Squadrons would co-operate. In peacetime, of course, the Harriers disperse well away from farms and villages, but in war every location offering cover from hostile reconnaissance and a space for a short take-off and vertical recovery would be potentially a Harrier air base.

Peacetime training for the Harrier force, therefore, presents all the airborne challenges met by more conventional aircraft plus the need for mastery of the VTOL techniques and the task of locating, preparing and operating from remote sites. Not only must the aircraft be well hidden, but space must be found for fuel, weapons, signals and living complexes essential to the support of the Harriers in the field. Sometimes grass or woodland clearings need to be strengthened by steel strips but in a real emergency much greater use would be made of country lanes and roads. When the sites are fully prepared, and the Harriers are at stand-by in them, they are virtually invisible to ordinary aerial reconnaissance although infra-red line-scan equipped aircraft would pick them out, if they were flying in the right area in the first place.

At war, the Harrier crews in their cockpits would await the telebrief from squadron or site operations, passed by secure channel from the joint Army-Support Operation Centre. They would have received continual intelligence up-dates giving the positions of both sides now locked in combat on the ground. Prefixed by the individual aircraft call-sign the 'immediate' request would tersely describe the target: 'armour at such-and-such a grid reference', or 'line search on road a, b, c'. The pilot might then swiftly enter the appropriate co-ordinates in his inertial navigation attack system or, more likely, simply check his maps for a point which he would almost certainly know off by heart after many hours of flying over the ground, and prepare to move out. Camouflage net would be thrown back, the

Harrier would move out from the trees, turn down the lane or field and be airborne in a very few seconds. Transiting at perhaps 150ft, with four cluster weapons, the pilot might be given a target up-date by the forward air controller down below with the ground forces. In a fast-moving battle it is obviously essential that the pilot should receive the most accurate and up-to-date information. Taking advantage of his high speed and knowledge of the terrain to fly at very low altitude, he would take the forward air defences by surprise and be over his target less than 20 minutes after the request for his assistance had been made. With the cluster bomb units he has no need to climb to make a shallow dive attack; simply one fast pass and a large area of ground is spattered with bomblets able to severely damage all kinds of ground vehicles. Then back to the hide, still very low level, perhaps using the differential vector thrust to evade enemy interception. Each aircraft or pilot could be expected to fly up to five such missions a day providing considerable assistance to hard-pressed, and probably outnumbered, ground forces.

The Harrier concept of operations is therefore quite unique. On the one hand forward deployment permits very fast reaction to requests for assistance to ground forces. But also, should the Warsaw Pact ever contemplate a pre-emptive attack on NATO's air power, it would be aware that it would have no guarantee of knocking out, or even grounding, the Harrier force. Indeed, it would have no idea where to look for it. So the ability to operate from dispersed sites is not just of offensive value, but by reducing the aircraft's vulnerability and by complicating the Warsaw Pact's own offensive calculations, the Harrier force clearly makes a powerful contribution to deterrence.

Out of Theatre Operations

It is tempting to believe that if the Warsaw Pact had any doubts about Harrier's versatility and effectiveness they could have been dissolved by the aircraft's performance in the South Atlantic in May 1982. Prior to that period, No 1 Squadron at RAF Wittering had trained to play its part, with the Jaguars of the Coltishall wing, in the Allied

Harrier in Germany

Harrier makes a special contribution to the deterrent value of air power because of its dispersed forward deployment – no Warsaw Pact commander would know where to strike at its bases, or would know from where a counter-punch would come.

Below:
Question: which side of the road does a Harrier drive on in Germany? *Crown copyright photo by SAC Mitch Mitchell*

Above:
How will the enemy know where to look? Two Harriers taxi out prior to a shortrun take-off somewhere in the German forests. *Crown copyright photo by SAC Pete Boardman*

Command Europe Mobile Force. It deployed regularly to Norwegian airfields where its Harriers could demonstrate their ability to operate from remote sites or makeshift runways. Its operational methods and equipment closely resemble those of the Gutersloh wing but its area of deployment in the event of conflict in Europe would be likely to be much wider.

No 1 Squadron was formed in 1912 from the balloons, airships and kites of No 1 Airship Company of the Air Battalion of the Royal Engineers. Since then it has won battle honours on the Western Front in World War 1, the North-West Frontier of India, Iraq, France in 1939/40, the Battle of Britain – where the squadron flew Hurricanes from Tangmere and Northolt throughout the battle – and finally as a long range escort squadron to daylight bombing raids against Germany. In July 1969 it became the first operational squadron in the world to fly vertical take-off fighters and pioneered offensive support to ground forces from dispersed sites close to the potential battlefield. In 1982 it was deployed in an area, and operated from sites, quite undreamed of by either planners or pilots. Almost a year later, the CO of the Squadron during the Falklands War, Wg Cdr Peter Squire DFC, AFC, explained to an audience of the Royal Aeronautical Society how his Harriers came to be involved and what they contributed. The following extracts are taken from his address:

'Although based in UK, No 1 (F) Squadron would always deploy elsewhere in times of tension or war. It is declared to NATO as a reinforcement squadron with options ranging from North Norway to much warmer bases on the southern flank. Although it is totally dependent on airlift for deployment the squadron must be capable of full operations from "bare base", that is to say without any form of host nation assistance. On deployment, therefore, the squadron's peacetime establishment is heavily supplemented by specialist sub-units. These include the army engineers, affectionately known as sappers, who have the job of carrying out whatever field engineering tasks are required. These will range from the building of aircraft hides to the laying of metal runways and taxiways. Also in support we have a specialist logistic unit, which is responsible for the provision of fuel. Finally we take specialist communications and catering personnel. Because of this capability of bare-base operations, the squadron has something of a reputation as a "go anywhere outfit" and it was not surprising that we should become involved in Operation "Corporate", although if anyone had told me in March of last year that within two months we would be fighting a war from an aircraft carrier some 8,000 miles from home, I frankly would not have believed them.

Preparation
A warning order issued on 8 April told the squadron to prepare for operations from a carrier as replacements for Sea Harrier attrition losses.

'Modification of the aircraft was the first task. A number of pure navalisation modifications were required; these included putting shackles on the outriggers for lashing down, anti-corrosion treatment, modification to the engine limiting system and the fitting of specialist transponder equipment to assist recoveries to the carrier in bad weather. The Air Force Harrier (and from now on I will refer to it as the GR3) was bought as an attack aircraft with

Above:
A Harrier of No 3 Squadron in its forest hide.
Crown copyright photo by SAC Pete Boardman

Right:
Take-off from a forest road by a Harrier of No 4 Squadron.

only integral guns for self-defence. If we were to be used to replace Sea Harrier, a better air defence capability would be required and so within a few days of receiving the initial warning order, both industry and the Service were working flat out in order to give the aircraft an air-to-air missile fit. Thanks to a great deal of effort and ingenuity our aircraft were equipped, and the system proved and tested within 2½ weeks.

'Whilst the modification programme was being carried out, nominated pilots went through an intensive work-up programme; this included realistic air combat training, air-to-air missile firing, of which none of the pilots had any previous experience, operational weapon delivery profiles, ultra low flying and initiation into the ski-jump club . . .

'The helicopters were loaded in the UK but the GR3s and Sea Harriers were flown to Ascension. The GR3s were able to accomplish this 4,000-mile leg in one hop, thus creating new milestones in single seat ferry flight times of over nine hours. Once at Ascension the aircraft were flown on to the *Atlantic Conveyor* and tightly parked in the "aircraft hide", which had been created between the walls of containers. The aircraft had been "bagged" to give added protection against salt water.

'With a total of 14 Harriers and 10 helicopters embarked

this was a very valuable target and, during the passage south, one Sea Harrier was kept at a high state of readiness for air defence duties against a shadower type aircraft. For this purpose tanker support was also available to give the Sea Harrier extra radius of action. The very use of a container ship as a carrier of aircraft, let alone the ability to mount albeit limited offensive operations from it, is once again a hallmark of the Harrier's enormous flexibility.

'Having left Ascension on the evening of 7 May, the *Atlantic Conveyor* in company with other ships of the amphibious group made a rendezvous with the Task Force on 18 May and the Harriers were transferred to the two carriers, 10 to *Hermes* and four to *Invincible.* All the GR3s went to *Hermes* and, although none of my eight pilots had ever operated from a ship before, after just one day of work-up training the squadron flew its first operational sortie on 20 May.

Operations
'In the 2½ weeks between the arrival of the Task Force in the Tez and our arrival, no Sea Harriers had been lost in air combat and so, instead of being replacements, the GR3s were used as reinforcements and dedicated to the attack role. In this capacity we carried out the full gambit of offensive air support missions, ranging from offensive counter air to close air support and armed reconnaissance.

'The aims of the offensive counter air missions were twofold; firstly to deny the use of Stanley airfield and the various outlying strips and secondly to destroy aircraft in the open. Laydown type deliveries were flown against a number of the strips such as Goose Green and Dunnose Head, whilst against the runway at Stanley a great variety of profiles were used . . . Although the runway remained open to Hercules and Pucara type aircraft the Argentinians were not able to use the airfield as a forward operating base for fighter bomber-aircraft and that was the Task Force's main concern.'

'For its other attack tasks, the GR3 carried and delivered a variety of weapons, including cluster bombs, 2in rockets, 1,000lb bombs and, in due course, the laser-guided bomb. The cluster bomb had a marked effect against troops in defence positions. This was particularly true in the battle for Goose Green where the missions flown in close support of the 2nd Parachute Regiment had a significant effect on the outcome of that battle.

'It was also a highly effective weapon against storage areas such as fuel and against helicopters caught on the ground. Regrettably the full potential of the LGB could not be made use of until just one day before the ceasefire. It was not until then that the laser target markers were positioned at the right time and place. However, four bombs delivered from loft profiles achieved two direct hits on pinpoint targets and served notice on the Argentinians that we now had a weapon of extreme accuracy.

'The GR3 is also capable of carrying a reconnaissance pod equipped with a fan of five cameras, which give horizon to horizon cover. Using this capability and the organic processing facilities within *Hermes,* the GR3 was able to find concentrations of enemy defensive positions and other lucrative targets.

'Shortly after the landings in San Carlos Water, a Harrier forward operations base was built close to one of

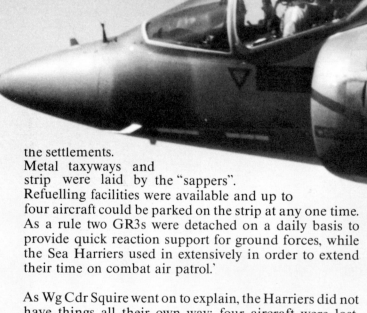

the settlements.
Metal taxyways and
strip were laid by the "sappers".
Refuelling facilities were available and up to
four aircraft could be parked on the strip at any one time.
As a rule two GR3s were detached on a daily basis to
provide quick reaction support for ground forces, while
the Sea Harriers used in extensively in order to extend
their time on combat air patrol.'

As Wg Cdr Squire went on to explain, the Harriers did not
have things all their own way: four aircraft were lost,
including three to enemy ground fire. It would appear
however that Harrier tactics of fast, low flight reduced the
threat from shoulder-fired SAMS considerably. What the
Wing Commander did not choose to emphasise was the
feat of a handful of RAF Harrier pilots, led by himself,
making their first carrier deck landing in the uncertain
waters of the South Atlantic. The 'lucky' ones simply
transferred from the *Atlantic Conveyor* to *Hermes*; those less
fortunate who brought out the replacement aircraft, had,
as the Wing Commander wryly observed, '8½ hours to
prepare for their first ever deck landing.' With good reason
did he conclude his address with the observation, 'The

Harrier may
not be ideal for every role,
but it has proved beyond
any doubt that it is a highly
effective weapons platform
with almost unlimited flexibility.'

Subsequently a Harrier detachment was
established at RAF Stanley, manned
by aircrew and groundcrew on rotation
from Wittering and Gutersloh. Now however the
GR3s were also equipped with Sidewinders, thereby
adding air defence to their previous all-round offensive
abilities. Forward operating bases were regularly used in
other parts of the islands so that should the Argentinians
ever decide to make a second call, they could no more
expect to catch all the Harriers on their home base than
could Warsaw Pact forces in an attack on Gutersloh.

Nor were the lessons of Harrier operations to be

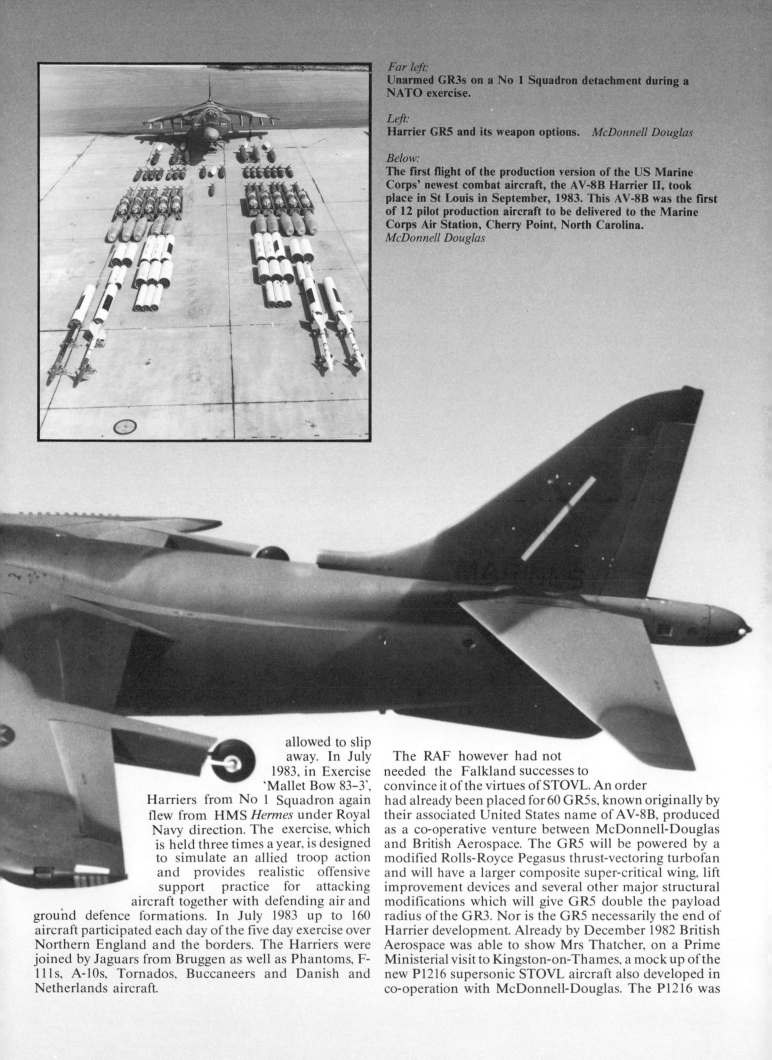

Far left:
Unarmed GR3s on a No 1 Squadron detachment during a NATO exercise.

Left:
Harrier GR5 and its weapon options. *McDonnell Douglas*

Below:
The first flight of the production version of the US Marine Corps' newest combat aircraft, the AV-8B Harrier II, took place in St Louis in September, 1983. This AV-8B was the first of 12 pilot production aircraft to be delivered to the Marine Corps Air Station, Cherry Point, North Carolina.
McDonnell Douglas

allowed to slip away. In July 1983, in Exercise 'Mallet Bow 83–3', Harriers from No 1 Squadron again flew from HMS *Hermes* under Royal Navy direction. The exercise, which is held three times a year, is designed to simulate an allied troop action and provides realistic offensive support practice for attacking aircraft together with defending air and ground defence formations. In July 1983 up to 160 aircraft participated each day of the five day exercise over Northern England and the borders. The Harriers were joined by Jaguars from Bruggen as well as Phantoms, F-111s, A-10s, Tornados, Buccaneers and Danish and Netherlands aircraft.

The RAF however had not needed the Falkland successes to convince it of the virtues of STOVL. An order had already been placed for 60 GR5s, known originally by their associated United States name of AV-8B, produced as a co-operative venture between McDonnell-Douglas and British Aerospace. The GR5 will be powered by a modified Rolls-Royce Pegasus thrust-vectoring turbofan and will have a larger composite super-critical wing, lift improvement devices and several other major structural modifications which will give GR5 double the payload radius of the GR3. Nor is the GR5 necessarily the end of Harrier development. Already by December 1982 British Aerospace was able to show Mrs Thatcher, on a Prime Ministerial visit to Kingston-on-Thames, a mock up of the new P1216 supersonic STOVL aircraft also developed in co-operation with McDonnell-Douglas. The P1216 was claimed to be 1½ times larger than the GR5 with both supersonic speed and increased manoeuvrability. There seems little doubt that if the MoD so disposes its priorities, and if government is prepared to encourage further STOVL development, the RAF could be involved in STOVL operations for many years to come.

Reconnaissance
Since the earliest days of military flight there has been a close connection between offensive operations and the reconnaissance which has invariably preceded them. The provision of general military intelligence remains the responsibility of a variety of agencies and systems, but the timely acquisition of information about enemy dispositions, movements, readiness, post-combat deterioration, etc, is very much the function of aerial reconnaissance. In addition there is now the mysterious and highly classified world of ELINT, the acronym for electronic intelligence. Eavesdropping on the radio communications and radar frequencies used by a potential opponent can provide valuable information about his mode of operations and enable one's own anti-radiation missiles, or other active and passive electronic countermeasures, to be accurately programmed before hostilities are joined. In February 1984 for example an article in the London *Economist* suggested that the Shrike anti-radiation missiles supplied to the RAF for use in the 'Black Buck' Vulcan attacks on the Falklands radars came already programmed with the Argentinian radar wavelengths. Such information can be provided by satellites and drones as well as by manned aircraft such as the USAF's SR-71 Blackbird and its EC-135s.

A rare glimpse of RAF activity in this esoteric area was afforded by Air Marshal Sir Peter Harding, Vice Chief of the Air Staff, when he visited the Electronic Warfare Operations Support Establishment (EWOSE) on 8 October 1982. The unit had been formed 12 months previously to be responsible for 'maximising the operational effectiveness of Electronic Warfare systems and specifically for reprogramming the new generation of software controlled systems shortly to enter service for Tornado and Nimrod.' Sir Peter was subsequently quoted as observing that 'before the South Atlantic conflict EWOSE was a new unit known mainly to a group of specialists. In the aftermath it was clear that EWOSE had won its spurs.' At the height of the Falklands war the Establishment was producing 24 copies weekly, each of 600 pages of classified printouts describing the South Atlantic electronic environment, reflecting acquired intelligence on the enemy and variations in friendly electronics disposition. Close co-operation between EWOSE and the Royal Navy had been of great value to the Task Force.

The PR Squadrons
In the RAF there are now two specialised tactical photo reconnaissance squadrons, both equipped with Jaguar GR1s: No 41 at Coltishall and No 2 at Laarbruch. No 41 shares the NATO reinforcement taks of the other two squadrons at Coltishall and has a long fighter tradition. Formed at Gosport in 1916 it has served almost entirely in the UK. It was also heavily engaged in the Battle of Britain, relieving No 54 Squadron at Hornchurch at the beginning of September. Plt Off E. S. Lock was, with 17 kills, one of the highest scoring pilots of the battle. No 2 Squadron was

formed in 1912 at Farnborough, and in the person of Second Lieutenant W. B. Rhodes Moorhouse won the first VC for the Royal Flying Corps in April 1915. Since 1939 the Squadron has operated almost entirely in the photo reconnaissance role. In due course it will be re-equipped at Laarbruch with the reconnaissance variant of the Tornado GR1.

Both Jaguar squadrons can operate in either the offensive support or the reconnaissance roles. When equipped for the latter their aircraft carry a centre-line pod containing five optical cameras and one infra-red one which are synchronised with the aircraft's NAVWASS. The infra-red photography defeats traditional camouflage by registering the heat impressions of vehicles, aircraft, buildings or indeed any other reason for temperature differentials on the ground within its focal range. Photography can be supplemented by pilot visual reports which can be relayed as an in-flight report once the aircraft is heading for home. The art of the recce pilot therefore demands not only extremely accurate navigation and low level flying skills but the ability to see, recognise, note or memorise, analyse and relate a considerable amount of detail in a very few seconds. When the Jaguar returns to base, its films can be unloaded and processed in an adjacent Reconnaissance Intelligence Centre within 12 minutes, even when all the supporting groundcrew are working in NBC kit. The aircraft pilot joins the photo interpretation team, and the information requested by the ground forces will be en route to them in little over 30 minutes after the Jaguar has landed. As computerised equipment is increasingly used those times will be progressively reduced until the provision of 'real time' information from airborne aircraft, via an intelligence fusion centre to the user on the ground, will be timed in seconds rather than minutes. The significance of that kind of timely intelligence to a commander in the field needs no exaggeration.

Until the beginning of the decade photo reconnaissance was also provided by two Canberra squadrons: No 39 and No 13, flying PR9s and PR7s. Now the long tradition of the PR Canberra is maintained by a handful of PR9s flown by No 1 Photo Reconnaissance Unit at RAF Wyton, carrying out mapping and associated tasks for the MoD, as well as odd jobs as diverse as surveying the route for the Falklands Flypast over London in October 1982 or locating the source of losses in underground heating pipes by use of the infra-red linescan equipment. No 1 PRU also works closely with other units at Wyton in support of the nearby Joint Air Reconnaissance Centre at Brampton.

The Offensive Capability
All in all, the offensive capability of British air power has been, and continues to be, progressively enhanced with the introduction into service of the Tornado and the improvements to the Jaguar and Harrier forces. Its ability with its NATO allies to penetrate enemy defences, and to locate and destroy a wide range of targets presents an increasingly difficult problem to those who might seek to launch an offensive which would lean very heavily on carefully co-ordinated pre-planned operations and regular, reliable reinforcement by air and land. In peacetime, the counter-offensive capability of the RAF is a major contributor to deterrence; in war it would play a powerful part in checking an aggressor.

Photo-Reconnaissance Jaguars

Offensive support is not the only role in which the Jaguar operates. An important task in support of offensive operations is that of photo-reconnaissance, and Nos 2 and 41 Squadrons can perform this in addition to their strike operations.

Top:
Not a Zebra, but a Jaguar from No 41 Squadron crossing the runway-road intersection in Gibraltar.

Above:
A frozen lake? Or a frozen airfield? A Jaguar of No 41 Squadron awaits its next photo-recce details.

5 Air Mobility and In-flight Refuelling

The perennial numerical superiority of in-place Warsaw Pact ground forces over the NATO troops facing them has for many years now placed a high premium on the Western alliance's ability to reinforce extremely swiftly. Air mobility therefore lies at the heart of NATO's conventional deterrent posture and, should that policy ever fail, would have a critical contribution to make to NATO's defensive war-fighting capability. But Britain also retains widespread commitments beyond Europe, as the events in spring of 1982 forcibly reminded us, and British air power must be prepared, while concentrating on the European theatre, to provide air mobility to ground, sea and other force units over a large part of the globe. The responsibility for that air mobility rests with the fixed and rotary wing aircraft of the RAF's transport squadrons, increasingly supported by in-flight refuelling provided by an unusual variety of aircraft.

The Hercules Force

The heart of the Royal Air Force's tactical transport force is at Royal Air Force Lyneham in Wiltshire, the home of the Hercules fleet. The Hercules entered RAF service in 1967, replacing the Hastings and Beverley. It shows every sign of becoming the Dakota of the 1980s because of its astonishing versatility. Although it has a 4,600-mile range with a 20,000lb payload and cruises at 345mph, it can also operate comfortably from short unprepared strips. Its rugged construction and high serviceability rate makes it an excellent tactical transport. The C Mk1 is similar to the Hercules C-130E used by the USAF but the four 4,910shp Allison turboprop engines are rather more powerful than those in the 130E. It can carry 92 fully-armed troops or a variety of vehicles: three Ferret Scout cars plus 30 troops or two Scout helicopters or a Saladin armoured car plus a Ferret. In parachute dropping its roller conveyor system facilitates the despatch of heavy platforms in excess of 30,000lb. Sixty-two paratroops can be dropped from the fuselage side-doors or 40 from the rear load ramp. When used for casualty evacuation it can carry 74 stretchers.

The major units at Lyneham are No 242 OCU and Nos 24, 30, 47 and 70 Squadrons. No 242 OCU is responsible for the training of all five aircrew members of the Hercules: the two pilots, navigator, air engineer and air loadmaster. The complete course lasts for five months comprising ground, school, simulator and flying phases. The co-pilot, for example, flies some 20 hours general handling and instrumental flying plus another 36 on 'route' training. A further 36 hours are spent by the entire converting crew in one of three simulators which can reproduce a range of situations from emergency drills to approaches into difficult airfields, such as Katmandu in Nepal.

On successfully 'converting' to the Hercules, the crew

Below:
Airbridge north and south: Ascension Island. *Author*

members join one of the four operational squadrons. All have long and distinguished records as transport units but now discharge slightly differing roles. No 24, which was formed as a fighter squadron in 1915, has flown all the RAF's major transport aircraft since 1920, and No 30, which was expressly formed for overseas service in 1914 but flew fighter operations in World War 2 before becoming a transport squadron in 1947, undertake route flying tasks only. Nos 47, a transport squadron which flew in the Berlin Airlift and which has flown Hercules since 1968, and 70, which dropped paratroops on Port Said in 1956 during a 55-year unbroken period of service in the Middle East, also have transport support tasks. These include low level operations by day and night, dropping men and equipment by parachute, and airborne assault techniques. Before crews undertake these roles, they must return to the OCU for a further specialised three-week course. Thereafter, they will work with the parachute battalions of the British Army, both in day-to-day training and in airborne assault exercises which take place annually in the United Kingdom and NATO-wide in Europe. Such exercises may be straightforward missions in which a stream of Hercules flies direct to a dropping zone (DZ) or they may, on the other hand, call for low level diversionary routeing through or around simulated air-to-air or ground-to-air defences. Carefully selected crews may be tasked to work with units of the Special Air Services or the Special Boat Service of the Royal Marines. Such air support is the descendant of the work in World War 2 with special operations forces and clearly calls for the highest navigational and flying skills in a variety of demanding environments worldwide.

The Hercules Force discharges three major tasks: support of NATO, support of national commitments and assistance to other nations. NATO operations could include the support of the ACE Mobile Force or the UK Mobile Force on its deployment to the mainland of Europe. Since 1982 of course, the national commitment to the South Atlantic has figured very prominently in its

daily operations, but the orientation of natural defence policy remains unchanged and so therefore do the Lyneham wing's priorities. In September 1984 for example, the wing made a major contribution to Exercise 'Lionheart 84', a major NATO reinforcement exercise in which some 50,000 men and women of the Regular and Reserve forces were moved to the continent, to join troops from several allied nations in wide ranging field training exercises. This operation was even larger than its predecessor in 1980, Exercise 'Crusader', when the Hercules flew troops, supported the deployments of the UK-based Harrier, Jaguar and helicopter squadrons and dropped paratroops directly into the combat zone near the Weser canal. Such activities, albeit on a smaller scale, comprise the first priority of the Hercules force all the year round.

The massive airlift operated over the South Atlantic in 1982 deserves full description, but at the beginning of the decade air mobility had in an unobtrusive way made a major contribution to a peaceful political settlement: to facilitate the progress of Zimbabwe to independence.

After the Lancaster House agreements of 1979, it was essential that the Commonwealth Monitoring Force should be swiftly deployed and that the Patriotic Front guerillas should be adequately supplied in their new assembly areas. The Hercules mounted over 250 sorties, lifting 5,000 passengers and over 2½ million pounds of freight of which three-quarters of a million was air-dropped because no other means of resupply was feasible. The tactical support sorties were flown by crews from Nos

Top:
Chinook helicopter of No 18 Squadron airlifting an Argentinian Pucara during the big airfield clean-up at Stanley.
Sgt Maurice R. Lockey RAF

Above:
Casevac exercise in RAFG.

47 and 70 Squadrons. The weather was frequently poor, with rain, poor visibility and a cloud base of 200–300ft. Moreover, there was, from the outset, the possibility that Patriotic Front guerillas would use their SAM-7s, RPG-7 rocket launchers or 7.62mm machine guns against the Hercules. In the event, one Hercules did take a 7.62mm round which narrowly missed the liquid oxygen supply and all flying had to be planned on the assumption of a

hostile threat from the ground. Transit speeds were in the order of 260kt indicated air speed at below 200ft. Airdrops were made into clearings as small as half a football field and often surrounded by trees, minefields, rocks and other obstacles. Some of the Hercules had their undercarriages strengthened to facilitate short, unmade-strip landings and take-offs which quickly became commonplace in the exercise. Navigation was made more difficult by the need to improvise maps and charts and by the scarcity of prominent features in unfamiliar terrain. Despite these problems the Commonwealth Monitoring Force was deployed within the three days which had been requested and the Patriotic Front guerilla assembly areas were all resupplied even though on occasions the Hercules were flying five sorties a day in very bad weather. The extremely high standards of efficiency in the Hercules fleet were amply demonstrated.

The South Atlantic
Less than three years later, those high standards were to be given their most rigorous test since the demands placed on the old Transport Command by the Berlin Airlift of 1948–49. On 3 April, less than 24 hours after the Argentine invasion of the Falklands, the first Hercules to participate in Operation 'Corporate' left Lyneham to establish a RAF airhead at Wideawake Field on Ascension Island. The Lyneham station commander at the time, Gp Capt Clive Evans, who was subsequently awarded the CBE for his role of commander of the Hercules fleet, later observed that he had initially been asked to provide 'a small number of aircraft'. Indeed, the team from the UK Mobile Air Movements squadron flown down in the first Hercules expected to 'offload up to 13 Hercules' to support the Task Force. By the end of hostilities, the movements teams (now reinforced well beyond the initial six men) had processed 5,895 passengers and 13,970lb of freight. Total flying time in the airlift exceeded 15,000 hours, most of that by the Hercules fleet.

On 18 June a Hercules flown by a No 70 Squadron crew, skippered by Flt Lt Terry Locke, established a new Hercules endurance record of 28hr 4min, on a round trip of 6,800 nautical miles from Wideawake to Sapper Hill in the Falklands and return. Yet on the 3 April the maximum range of a Hercules with a normal payload had been only in the region of 4,500 nautical miles, depending on the usual weight/height/speed/wind factors. The gap was bridged as a result of a remarkable combination of air staff reaction, engineering improvisation and whole-hearted civilian co-operation. First, the engineers at Lyneham devised and fitted an auxiliary fuel tank in the forward cabin, but it quickly became obvious that even this speedy 'mod' was insufficient, and on 15 April Marshalls of Cambridge (Engineering) Ltd began to design a complete probe system which would eventually equip 20 of the Hercules C Mk 1s. The first installation was test flown on 28 April, delivered to Boscombe Down on the 29th, coupled three times with a Victor tanker, and delivered to Lyneham on 5 May. Meanwhile No 242 OCU had begun a joint aircrew training programme with the Marham specialists and the first AAR-equipped Hercules reached Wideawake on 12 May. The first reported long range air refuelling flight to the South Atlantic took place four days later when vital stores and six paratroops were dropped to HMS *Antelope* in a round trip of 6,300 miles

'Volant Rodeo 82'

This annual tactical airlift competition has always been popular with RAF representatives – and in 1982 the Hercules of Lyneham Wing were Best Allied Team and finished second in the Best Overall Wing award.

Top:
The Galloping Lady marks the beginning of Exercise 'Volant Rodeo 82'. *Sgt Maurice R. Lockey RAF*

Above:
Accuracy supply drop during the 'Volant Rodeo' competition in the USA. *Sgt Maurice R. Lockey RAF*

Below:
Bunkered? No, a Lyneham Hercules preparing to take off to do a short-field landing at Fort Bragg Falcon dropping zone. *Sgt Maurice R. Lockey RAF*

lasting 24hr 5 min. Subsequently Flt Lt Harold Burgoyne and Sqn Ldr Max Roberts of No 47 Squadron's Special Forces Flight were awarded the Air Force Cross for still classified 'clandestine operations'. By 3 June the Hercules force had flown 10,000 hours in Operation 'Corporate', and despite the primitive and hazardous operational environment, without loss or serious damage to a single aircraft.

Since September 1982 Hercules on detachment from Lyneham have maintained the 13-hour airbridge from Wideawake to Stanley with air-to-air refuelling support, described later in the chapter. By the end of March 1983 the wing had made more than 850 flights, carrying over 18 million pounds of freight between Lyneham and the South Atlantic. Yet despite this considerable addition to the station's task, it was still possible to detach an aircraft to compete in the annual 'Volant Rodeo' tactical airlift competition at Pope AFB in North Carolina. In 1982 the RAF team defeated the 29 other Allied contestants to win the Best Allied Team and the Best Security Police awards, tied for first place in the Maintenance competition and finished second Best Overall Wing. All in all, Gp Capt Evans had every reason to be proud of the men and women whom he commanded at Lyneham.

In a few short weeks the traditional distinction between a tactical and strategic transport aircraft was permanently blurred in the RAF. Hitherto the VC10s of No 10 Squadron had sole residual claim to the title for a strategic role that had seemed to be declining with the progressive British withdrawal from imperial responsibilities during the previous generation. Both the Short Belfasts – ironically involved in 'Corporate' in their new civilian colours – and the Bristol Britannias had left RAF squadron service as defence policy concentrated on our NATO commitment. Nevertheless, the unrefuelled range of the VC10s with their payload of 150 troops or 54,000lb of freight made them also a vital component of the airlift to Ascension. In addition, equipped in their casualty evacuation fit, they flew home 568 casualties from Uruguay where they had disembarked from the hospital ships after transfer from the war zone. It is a tribute to the skill of the RAF doctors, nurses and medical assistants that no patient's condition deteriorated during their 7,000-mile flight home.

Moreover, just as a tactical transport can be stretched over extended distances, so the longer range VC10 can be used as a shuttle in European exercises or reinforcement,

as it was in both 'Crusader 80' and 'Lionheart 84'. Large scale reinforcement will always be a combined services task, because there can be no substitute for naval transport for large scale tonnage and large numbers of men, as the Falklands Task Force amply demonstrated. Nevertheless the work of the Hercules and VC10s illustrates why flexibility of air power has reached the status of a cliché: a well worn expression but well worn because it is a frequently proven truth.

The Queen's Flight

Happily, one RAF organisation did not have to be diverted to the South Atlantic: The Queen's Flight at RAF Benson. The Flight is equipped with three twin-turboprop Andover CC Mk 2 aircraft and two Westland Wessex HCC4 helicopters. It is manned by 175 officers and men under the command of the Captain of the Queen's Flight, Air Vice Marshal J. de M. Severne MVO, OBE, AFC, FBIM who was appointed in January 1982. The Flight was formed as The King's Flight at RAF Hendon in 1936 by King Edward VIII. During World War 2 it formed the nucleus of No 161 Squadron engaged on special duties which included the dropping of agents and equipment to resistance forces behind enemy lines in occupied Europe. Today the Flight flies members of the Royal Family, senior Ministers of the Crown, Chiefs of Staff and visiting Heads of State. The Duke of Edinburgh and the Prince of Wales, both qualified pilots, frequently fly the aircraft themselves.

The Wessex helicopters, usually employed for shorter journeys of up to 200 miles, can be expected to remain in service, like the other RAF Wessex, at least until the end of the decade. Their serviceability is maintained by rigid maintenance schedules which require the groundcrew to work until the aircraft needed are serviceable, regardless of normal shift hours. Additional safeguards of reduced life replacement cycles for engines and other components ensure that only unacceptable weather conditions ever delay the beginning or the end of a Royal flight. Despite the long hours worked, there is never any shortage of volunteers for the five-year tour of duty at Benson.

The Andovers however will be replaced in the near future by two British Aerospace 146s similar to the ones at present conducting extensive flight trials with the RAF. They will offer greatly increased range and all-weather capability as well as retaining much of the short field performance which has made the Andover such a valuable aircraft on many Royal overseas tours in less developed regions. Although the Royal aircraft were not called upon in the 1982 conflict, the BAe 146s could in an emergency provide a valuable supplement to the rest of the RAF's transport fleet.

The less glamorous but equally hardworking communication squadrons of the RAF are also about to be modernised. No 32 Squadron at Northolt regularly transports distinguished passengers to various destinations in the UK and Western Europe while No 60, based at Wildenrath, performs similar duties in RAF Germany. It was announced in March 1983 that the venerable Pembrokes and Devons would be progressively withdrawn

Above:
A Hercules from the Lyneham wing: the provision of tactical mobility from UK to RAFG.
Crown copyright photo by SAC Pete Boardman

Right:
The communications squadrons at Northolt have often carried very important persons …

and their duties taken over by Andovers and British Aerospace HS125-700s. Four additional HS125-700s were ordered to join the earlier 125-500s which are being re-engined to 700 series standard. The programme was a further example of the comprehensive and cost effective enhancement of all segments of the fixed-wing air mobility force in this decade.

The Rotary Wing Element

While the distinction in the fixed-wing transport force between tactical and strategic air mobility has become somewhat blurred, the contribution of the RAF's support helicopter force lies squarely within the geographical confines of an operational theatre. Having said that however, the theatres are themselves located worldwide.

Headquarters of the helicopter force is at RAF Odiham in Hampshire, where No 240 OCU trains the aircrews for the Puma and Chinook squadrons. Further north at RAF Benson is the Wessex Training Unit.

The main function of the support helicopter squadrons is to provide battlefield mobility of troops and supplies and to support Harrier forward deployment.

The Pumas

No 33 Squadron operates Pumas at Odiham and was accompanied in that role by No 230 Squadron until the latter moved to Gutersloh in 1980. Its function is to provide tactical transport and battlefield support facilities for No 1 (British) Corps and, like the Harriers during a period of tension, it would deploy off base. Unlike its fixed-wing colleagues, No 230 Squadron originated in naval aviation, as part of the Royal Naval Air Service War Flight based at Felixstowe in World War 1. It became No 230 Squadron in 1918 and until 1957 had a distinguished maritime record which included support to Wingate's Chindits by flying to the Brahmaputra River and, after World War 2, contributing to the Berlin Airlift by flights to Lake Havel. It arrived at Gutersloh with its Pumas in late 1980.

The SA-330 Puma Mk 1 is a joint product of SNAIS and Westland. It is powered by two Turbomeca 111 C4 engines of 130shp each and can carry 16 troops or internal and external loads of up to 2,500kg. It has a maximum range of 390 miles and a cruising speed of 165mph.

In peacetime Pumas deploy for exercises in small numbers under camouflage in woods and near farm buildings from where they can swiftly provide logistic support, troop mobility, casualty evacuation, or with side-mounted machine guns they can operate as gunships. They are accompanied by an army officer who is usually an Army Air Corps pilot and a logistic expert who would act as a link between the Squadron and No 1 (British) Corps.

In addition to contributing to NATO exercises in the United Kingdom and on the mainland of Europe, the helicopter force also has purely national commitments. One detachment of Pumas is permanently deployed to Belize while another works with the security forces in Northern Ireland. The ability of the Puma to carry loads of up to 5,500lb as underslung cargo is of great value to the security forces. In addition to providing mobility for 16 fully-equipped troops it can lift vehicles, provisions or even a mundane concrete mixer from point to point,

Fit for a Queen

Below:
Secure for the night: BAe 146, during trials for selection as replacement aircraft for the Queen's Flight.
Crown copyright photo by Sgt John Stubbert

Above right:
XV732, a Wessex helicopter of the Queen's Flight.

Below right:
One of the three RAF Benson-based Queen's Fight Andover CC Mk 2s.

thereby denying terrorists a relatively soft target on the remote winding lanes near the border in South Armagh.

Until June 1973 the tiny central American territory of Belize was known as British Honduras; by then it had already received a promise of independence and was internally self-governing. But its 8,800 square miles are coveted by its much larger western neighbour, Guatemala. In 1975 Guatemala began to amass troops on the Belize border and reinforcement of Belize from the UK was required. Since then, British forces have been stationed in Belize as a deterrent to aggression and among them have been Harriers, helicopters and RAF Regiment units. In October 1975 three Pumas of No 33 Squadron were air-lifted to the territory, followed in November by six

Harriers of No 1 Squadron which were refuelled eight times in their flight across the Atlantic. These were then followed by an RAF Regiment detachment to provide airfield defence and in a very short time tension across the border lessened to such an extent that the Harriers were able to return to the United Kingdom. Regrettably, in July 1977, continued Guatemalan pressure and a repeat of the threatening gestures of two years previously prompted the United Kingdom Government to return the Harriers which, on their arrival sweep over Belize city, were greeted enthusiastically by the local population.

By 1984, although negotiations between Belize, Guatemala and the United Kingdom had again taken place, a force of 200 RAF servicemen in a British presence of just

over 2,000 remained to guarantee the small nation's integrity. The Harrier detachment was now shared between Nos 1, 3 and 4 Squadrons with four pilots on detachment at any one time. The air threat would come, if at all, from the small force of Guatemalan A-37s and the Harrier's responsibility would be to provide air defence of Belize Airport, keep open the air reinforcement routes and give close air support, reconnaissance and air cover to British ground forces. The Puma detachment, now the responsibility of No 230 Squadron, is to provide air mobility and tactical resupply to troops in an area where roads are few and movement on the ground is restricted by swamp and jungle. Regular strategic support is provided by the Lyneham Hercules wing and the VC10s of No 10 Squadron.

When the contribution of air power to national strategy is discussed its flexibility – the fact that it can discharge so many responsibilities with such speed and over such distances – is frequently stressed. Its use in Belize is a small but typical example. Aircraft whose primary responsibility is to contribute to the deterrent forces facing the Warsaw Pact were deployed several thousand miles away in a matter of hours, to a climate where temperatures of 100° and very high humidity are commonplace, to act as a token of the British Government's guarantee. Moreover, although as yet not tried in combat, junior officers must accept responsibility beyond those normally faced as a squadron pilot. Under the detachment commander they will supervise the flying programme, the engine tests, flight tests, supplies and combat survival. Whereas the RAF Regiment airmen with their Rapier surface-to-air missiles will be very obvious near the main airfield the Harriers will be deployed in the separate hides and the Pumas constantly range the hinterland. The result is a peace and domestic stability not shared by all the neighbours of Belize in an increasingly troubled Caribbean area.

The Puma force also contributed to Exercise 'Agila'. Six Pumas were airlifted by USAF C-5A Galaxy transports to Rhodesia and, while the Hercules were tasked with the heavy duties, the helicopters carried out the lighter air support tasks, casualty evacuation, and ferrying passengers between Salisbury and the various Patriotic Front assembly areas. In the four months of the detachment, the six helicopters flew 848 hours, carrying over 160,000lb of freight and 3,000 passengers. Despite the unfamiliar geographical conditions, the Pumas maintained a 97% serviceability rate throughout all sorties.

The Wessex Force
Although only the Pumas were deployed to Rhodesia, the longer serving Wessex participated in Exercise 'Crusader 80', bears the brunt of the detachment in Northern Ireland, and continues to provide tactical mobility to the British Army, both within NATO and in Hong Kong. Indeed, in 1981 the rotational detachment of helicopters from Odiham to Northern Ireland was replaced by the permanent positioning of No 72 Squadron. Although lacking the lifting power of the Puma, the twin-engined Wessex has a longer range and can carry seven stretchers, 15 troops or 3,600lb of freight and will continue to make a valuable contribution to tactical mobility for some time.

Across the other side of the world, an RAF presence is happily much more symbolic. There is no external threat to the Crown Colony of Hong Kong, now living harmoniously in the shadow of the Chinese Peoples' Republic, but there is nevertheless plenty of work to keep No 28 Squadron, equipped with Westland Wessex HC2s, fully occupied. Formed at Gosport in 1915, No 28 has spent all its operational service outside the UK. It flew in Italy in World War 1 and, since 1920, has operated in the Far East. It flew Lysanders, Hurricanes and Spitfires against the Japanese in Burma and moved to Hong Kong in 1949. It was successively equipped with Vampires, Venoms and Hunters at Kai Tak until assuming rotary wing duties with Whirlwind HAR 10s in 1968. In 1972 it received its Wessex HC2s. In 1978, because of the increasingly congested and restricted airfield facilities at Kai Tak, the eight helicopters of the Squadron moved across into the New Territories, just four miles from the Chinese border at RAF Sek Kong. It now contributes to the continual task of the colony's ground forces in intercepting the thousands of illegal immigrants who every year seek to reach urban Hong

Puma

Below:
A No 230 Squadron Puma on exercise in Bavaria.
Crown copyright photo by SAC Pete Boardman

Right:
Aid to the civil power: this No 230 Squadron Puma is giving a helping hand at Munster in West Germany.
Crown copyright photo by SAC Pete Boardman

Below right:
A Puma of No 33 Squadron on exercise.

Kong from mainland China. Rather than maintaining air surveillance it provides air mobility to the Army observation posts placed along the 22 miles of the colony's border, resupplying and rotating troops as well as evacuating casualties from positions which are frequently difficult to reach by land routes. Spotting illegal immigrants slipping across to the colony by sea is more difficult as the 55ft high speed launches tend to lose themselves among the hundreds of off-shore craft when a No 28 Squadron Wessex is in the area. Again, however, as in Belize, a small number of aircraft covers a wide area in peaceful support of a civil power and give a readily visible sign of British commitment.

One Wessex squadron, No 84 in Cyprus, can justifiably claim to be multi-role. Its primary established function is to provide search and rescue support to flying operations from its own base at Akrotiri, but in recent years it has been called upon for far more than that, operating in support of both the British forces in Cyprus, British Forces Lebanon and the United Nations force in Cyprus (UNFICYP). It is unique in several ways. It is the only RAF flying squadron permanently based in the Mediterranean area. Second, it is the only truly multi-role helicopter unit, employing most of the capabilities that a Wessex can provide. And it is the only RAF squadron to serve permanently in support of a United Nations force.

Until March 1982 the Squadron operated two flights of Whirlwind helicopters. 'A' Flight was based at RAF Akrotiri and provided search and rescue and communications services to the British forces. 'B' Flight was located at Nicosia International Airport and operated in support of UNFICYP. In March 1982 the Squadron was equipped with the Wessex and the two flights were merged into one single unit at RAF Akrotiri.

Because the island of Cyprus is 3,572 square miles in area and is about 90 miles (north–south) by 140 miles (east–west), the new-look squadron was grateful for the larger and faster aircraft which could provide the whole of the island with SAR cover from its base at RAF Akrotiri. The varied terrain is matched by the extremes of temperatures. In the summer months, on the 600 square mile Central Plain around the capital, Nicosia, the temperature is often in excess of +35°C, while in the winter months a helicopter crew taking off from Akrotiri in a balmy (by UK standards) +10°C finds itself 20 minutes later on the landing pad at Mount Olympus, 6,000ft above sea level, in temperatures of −10°C.

Over the years No 84 Squadron has built up a reputation for fast and efficient service in the search and rescue role. For example a mayday call was received from a Lebanese vessel, the *Scirrocco*. Its crew was abandoning ship 30 miles West of Paphos, after the ship's engines had failed and the ship had begun to take on water. Two helicopters of No 84 Squadron rescued the 15-man crew from their lifeboats.

Medical evacuations (Medevacs) are a part of the Squadron's service to the British and United Nations forces in Cyprus. Occasionally the Squadron is called upon to assist the Greek Cypriot and Turkish Cypriot authorities on the island (which have no SAR helicopters of their own), as well as victims of snake bits and scorpion stings, people suffering from appendicitis, fractures and divers' 'Bends', and expectant mothers who have to be taken to the Princess Mary's Hospital at RAF Akrotiri if they happen to live far away in Nicosia or the Eastern Sovereign Base Area.

The Squadron also carries VIPs and does much work for UNFICYP, it assists in troop training for the various contingents, as well as regular resupply runs to several of the Danish observations posts (OPs) in the United Nations buffer zone separating the Turkish forces in the north and the Greek Cypriot forces in the south. The rugged mountainous terrain in which these OPs are set is such that regular resupply runs of food and water would be difficult

Above:
No 230 Squadron Puma XW229 near its home base at Gütersloh. *Crown copyright photo by SAC Pete Boardman*

Below:
An eight-ship formation of No 28 Squadron Wessex over Shatin, New Territories, Hong Kong.

Right:
A Chinook of No 18 Squadron gives a Puma of No 33 Squadron a helping hand.

86

The One That Got Away

Above:

Chinook 'Bravo November' on board *Atlantic Conveyor* leaving England on her ill-fated voyage.

Below:

Work well done. After this preparation by RAF groundcrew on *Atlantic Conveyor* 'Bravo November' escaped the air attack and flew continuously throughout the conflict: the other Chinooks were lost.

and hazardous in winter by any transport other than the helicopter. The Wessex is the most practical way of evacuating injured or sick persons from the more remote OPs speedily and efficiently and with minimum distress to the patient. The Squadron also has a commitment to help with fire-fighting – moving fire crews and equipment, and evacuating casualties – when brush fires in the buffer zone get out of hand.

In early 1984 the Squadron supported the British contribution to the multi-national force in Lebanon. Flights to and from Beirut involved refuelling the Wessex from ships of the Royal Navy, the United States Navy, or the French Navy, a new dimension to No 84 Squadron's international commitments.

The Advent of the Chinook

In 1981 the support helicopter force was enlarged and strengthened by the entry into service of the Boeing Chinook HC-1. A mere list of Chinook's vital statistics does not convey the dramatic increase in capability which the new force conferred. The helicopter is able to carry over 20,000lb payload at a maximum speed of 175kt and has a range of 250 miles. It has three cargo hooks to allow it to deliver three separate underslung loads to different destinations and its interior cabin is 30ft long, 8ft 3in wide and 6ft 6in high. It can land on water and remain afloat at sea-state two for at least two hours when still weighing 36,000lb gross. But, in practical terms, these figures mean that Chinook could recover an unserviceable Harrier, or move 44 fully-armed troops, or 10 tons of ammunition or fuel, or a five-ton truck in all weathers by day or night, over a combat radius which covers all the territory under the wing of RAF Germany. Expressed another way, that is a range and payload combination almost four times greater than that of Puma. With internal long range fuel tanks its ferry range can be increased to 1,000 miles, conveying even greater flexibility for out-of-theatre deployment. In due course all the RAF's Chinooks will be fitted with glass-fibre blades to increase reliability, facilitate servicing and make the aircraft more resistant to battle damage, and will be fitted with radar warning receiver equipment. In fact, the Chinook was to have an early opportunity to demonstrate its impact on battlefield support, when four aircraft deployed south in May 1982 to participate in the Falklands landings. Disaster struck the detachment when the *Atlantic Conveyor* fell victim to Argentinian air power, hit by two Exocet missiles launched by Super Etendards probably aiming at HMS *Hermes*. Three of the four helicopters were not yet ready to take off and were lost with the ship. The fourth, 'Bravo November' of No 18 Squadron, was already airborne and escaped. It operated throughout the remainder of the campaign from a detachment at Port San Carlos. Despite the loss of all its support equipment on *Atlantic Conveyor,* 'Bravo November' logged more than 150 flying hours, carried a total of 1,500 troops, 600 tons of equipment and 650 prisoners of war. On one occasion it lifted 81 troops towards the battle zone, almost twice its normal limit. British troops, not always noted for sentimental attachment to RAF transport, christened 'Bravo November' 'The Flying Angel' in recognition of the invaluable support it had given them both before and after combat.

When peace returned to the Falklands much work remained to be done which could best be carried out by helicopters. Within 12 months the Chinook force, now numbered 1310 Flight, comprised six aircraft drawn from No 7 Squadron, formed at Odiham in September 1982, and No 18 Squadron, which was to move from Odiham to Gutersloh in May 1983. The Flight is now deployed at a 'permanent' portakabin site at Kelly's Garden near San Carlos Water. Its primary function is to provide swiftly reacting mobility to the ground forces should another Argentinian threat emerge, but meanwhile the aircraft are in constant demand not only for routine ship-to-shore movement of supply containers but also in deliveries to the many remote military sites scattered across a territory the size of Wales and far more inaccessible. Construction of the radar site on Mount Kent for example depended entirely on Chinook lift, as have two later radar stations built elsewhere on the islands.

In No 1310 Flight, squadron identity is temporarily submerged, but both Nos 7 and 18 Squadrons have distinguished histories. No 7 was the last RFC squadron to be formed before the outbreak of World War 1 – on 1 May 1914 – in which it discharged reconnaissance duties. Its most famous combat contribution was made from 1942 to 1945 when, first with Stirlings and then with Lancasters, it was pre-eminent in the Path Finder Force which led Bomber Command's night attacks against Germany's industrial heartland. From 1956 to 1962 it was equipped with Valiant B1s in the V-Force and, before re-forming with Chinooks, had flown some of the last of the RAFs

Canberras. No 18 squadron has had an equally distinguished and varied career. Since its formation at Northolt in 1915 it has flown fighters, light bombers, heavy bombers, transports and helicopters. It attacked the invasion barges in the Channel ports in 1940, enemy shipping in the Mediterranean from Malta in 1941 and gave support to the North African campaign thereafter. In 1947 it flew Dakotas in the Berlin Airlift and, after a spell as a bomber squadron with Canberras and Valiants, became a helicopter squadron in 1964.

Indeed, the activities of both Chinook squadrons and their recent theatres of operations indicate how aircraft designed for short range tactical activity can become the fingertips of the longer strategic arm. In 1983 Chinooks of Nos 7 and 18 Squadrons were moved swiftly to Akrotiri to provide support for the British peacekeeping force in the Lebanon. Their range and speed enabled them to wait discreetly in Cyprus well out of range of hostile action but able to resupply as quickly as required. Then, in February 1984, three Chinooks, helped by Sea Kings of 846 RNAS and Wessex of No 84 Squadrons, lifted 115 troops, 518 civilians and all the heavy equipment belonging to 'A' Squadron of the 16th/5th Lancers, including Ferret scout cars, four-ton lorries and armoured Land Rovers. Throughout the evacuation the Chinooks maintained 100% serviceability.

It is easy under such circumstances to concentrate on the operational achievement of the aircraft and crews and lose sight of the considerable value of their contribution to the diplomatic flexibility possessed by a British government which could depend on a speedy evacuation of troops, civilians and equipment to a secure sanctuary should either the need or inclination arise. This was a classic example of the contribution of air mobility in

Below:
Chinook and standby unit of three-mule power at Kelly's Garden, Falklands. *Author*

Above:
Preparing to lift a unit from No 63 Rapier Squadron of the RAF Regiment. *Crown copyright photo by SAC Pete Boardman*

Left:
Chinooks of No 18 Squadron providing unscheduled air lift to the Army.

peacetime to enhance the options available to statesman in a very complex and delicate situation.

Air-to-Air Refuelling
In the relatively short history of military aviation, the aircraft designer has always had to resolve a complex equation of aircraft size, weight, power and fuel capacity, quite apart from the intricacies of the detailed aerodynamic shape of his finished product. In that equation, fuel capacity has almost always been the dominant factor. The greater the fuel load the greater the endurance, but also the greater the weight, the larger the aircraft, the more powerful the engines – and the greater the fuel consumption: an awkward spiral to interrupt.

Since 1923 various attempts were made to refuel aircraft in flight, and in 1944 the Air Ministry actually issued a contract to convert 600 Lancasters and 600 Lincolns to the flight refuelling role, but the project was subsequently cancelled. In 1958 the Valiant B1 became the first RAF jet-engined tanker; in 1966 the first Victor K1 squadron formed at RAF Marham. Of the original three squadrons, No 214 was disbanded in 1977, but the others, Nos 55 and 57, have added additional chapters to already long and illustrious histories. No 55 Squadron was a unit in the 41st Wing of the Royal Flying Corps, the forerunner of the Independent Bombing Force which itself was the progenitor of the concepts and objectives of Bomber Command in World War 2. Between 1939 and 1945 No 55 Squadron operated mainly in the Middle East, flying 352 sorties for example during the first 10 days of the Battle of Alamein. After a period of disbandment it began its association with various marks of Victor in 1960. No 57 Squadron was formed at Copmanthorpe in 1916 and spent five months in France as a fighter squadron before re-equipping with DH4 bombers and establishing the pattern for its subsequent operations in World War 2 and beyond. It acquired its first Victor B1s in 1959 and its tankers in June 1966.

Above:
Victor K2 of No 55 Squadron at Ascension. *Author*

Below:
The other half of the Victor tanker team: the No 57 Squadron representation at Ascension. *Author*

Bottom:
It's all very strange: early Hercules air-to-air refuelling trials in 1982. *Crown copyright photo by A. Booth*

Airbridge Refuelling

Above:
The modified cargo door of the Hercules tanker at RAF Stanley.

Until 1982 the greater part of the Marham wing's activities were in support of interceptors of Fighter Command, later No 11 Group, and of various offensive aircraft. The Victor K2 carries a total of 128,000lb of fuel which is theoretically all transferable as it can itself be refuelled in flight. Its four Rolls-Royce Conway Mk 201 turbojets generate 80,000lb of static thrust and provide a

Above left:
Begin the approach . . . then move up into visual contact position . . . prepare to take up refuelling approach . . . beginning the move into position behind and slightly below the hose and drogue . . . the final approach to the drogue . . . Happiness Is . . . for the Hercules pilot, a steady 220kt, green lights and fuel flowing. *All photos by the author*

maximum unrefuelled range of 4,000 miles. By refuelling, Lightnings, Phantoms and Tornado F2s are enabled to mount combat air patrols several hundred miles off the British coast thereby making possible interception of hostile aircraft before they can reach their own air-to-

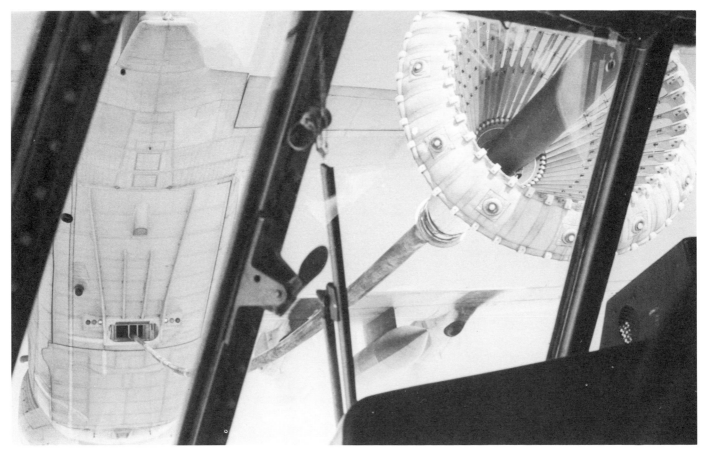

Above:
Even the Vulcan . . . XM571 of No 50 Squadron at RAF Waddington in AAR trials in 1982. *Crown copyright photo by A. Booth*

Left:
A Vulcan's eye view. *Photo by Flt Lt Mike Jenvey*

Below:
On the ground at Waddington – a No 50 Squadron Vulcan and drogue.

Above right:
The first VC10 air-to-air refueller undergoing trials, with starboard drogue extended; note the coloured stripes and lights to assist the crew of the receiving aircraft.

surface missile release point. In peacetime the aircraft can intercept and shadow the prowling 'Bear' well before it reaches British airspace, thereby emphasising how difficult its task would be in war. In May 1982, that allocation of effort was dramatically redirected. In a subsequent reflection on tanker operations generally, Air Marshal Sir Michael Knight, Air Member of the Air Force Board for Supply and Organisation, observed,

'In Royal Air Force terms, 1982 was the year of the tanker. Air-to-air refuelling, for so long the unsung adjunct of more glamorous missions, at last came into its own as a result of the South Atlantic operations, and the lessons learned will not be lost. Put simply the RAF's ability to carry out air-to-air refuelling (AAR) serves to increase the range, endurance and payload of its aircraft. Its acts as a "force extender" – even a "force multiplier".

As regards range, AAR not only enables both combat and support aircraft to go further but, more significantly in the case of recent operations in the South Atlantic, affords the ability to deploy aircraft rapidly – if necessary, without the use of staging bases.

'Increased endurance permits air defence aircraft to "loiter" while awaiting incoming enemy raids, thus allowing the air defence commander considerably greater flexibility in the use of his assets. More recently, the ability to refuel maritime reconnaissance aircraft has extended their patrol time, with the result that fewer aircraft have been used to carry out the tasks required.

'Finally, an increase in payload permits the operation of aircraft with higher weapon or freight loads. This can be of considerable value in operations from short or damaged runways, when aircraft may take off with a heavy payload and low fuel state, to be "topped up", once airborne, by a conveniently situated tanker.'

Quite simply, the long range air drops of vital equipment, bombing and surveillance missions so critical to the success of the Falklands campaign would have been impossible without the Victors from Marham. The Vulcan sorties for example required 50,000 gallons of in-flight fuel; 'Black Buck One' refuelled six times before the attack on Stanley airfield. Between 19 and 25 April three 14-hour maritime reconnaissance missions were flown by the Victors themselves, each requiring four tankers in support outbound and the same number for the recovery. The Victor role also demanded its own special kind of bravery. Unknown to the crew of Vulcan 'Black Buck One', a drama of potentially tragic conclusion had taken place behind it when a Victor broke its refuelling probe. The donor aircraft changed places with the damaged Victor, refuelled, made the RV with the Vulcan despite severe turbulence and violent storms but at the cost of leaving itself only enough fuel to reach a point 450 miles south of Ascension Island. Yet the captain was aware that if he broke radio silence before the Vulcan made its attack he would jeopardise the whole operation. In the event his coolness was rewarded when, confident that the Vulcan would have cleared the target area, he advised Ascension of his fuel state and a further Victor was scrambled to bring him safely back to base. For his 'Courage, leadership and outstanding flying ability', Sqn Ldr Bob Tuxford of No 55 Squadron was awarded the Air Force Cross.

But the cumulative demands of Operation 'Corporate' on the Victor force were enormous. Published accounts suggest that as many as 10 Victors were required to mount each 'Black Buck' mission, quite apart from the support required by the maritime reconnaissance Nimrods and the Harriers en route to the combat zone. During the hostilities Victors flew almost 600 sorties, and only six had to be aborted because of fuel transfer difficulties. Meanwhile, Buccaneers continued to contribute to air-to-air refuelling in the British Isles region in addition to their maritime offensive role, covering to a certain extent for the diversion of some of the Victors.

But still more refuelling capacity was required and in a very short time two new tanker types made their appearance. On 8 June a Hercules C Mk 1, fitted with four long range tanks in the cargo hold and a standard Flight Refuelling Ltd hose drogue unit (HDU), flew at Marshalls' airfield at Cambridge; while 10 days later a Vulcan B2 of No 50 Squadron flew with three tanks in its bomb bay and a similar HDU installed under its fuselage. Altogether, four Hercules were converted to C1Ks, and six Vulcans to K Mk 2s. The Hercules have proved invaluable in subsequent operations in the South Atlantic. Two, on station at RAF Stanley, allow both Harriers and Phantoms to fly extended combat air patrols. The other two sustain the regular Hercules airbridge between Wideawake and Stanley. For two years the Vulcan K2s of No 50 Squadron provided a most valuable addition to the air defence team, until 1984, when a new generation of tankers began to become operational, and they were finally withdrawn: the culmination of 30 years of Vulcan flying with the Royal Air Force.

In 1979 four second-hand VC10s were bought from Gulf Air, five Super VC10s from East African Airways and in 1981 a second batch of VC10s from British Airways. From these it was decided to construct a major addition to the Service's tanker force. In July 1983 the first converted VC10 K2 was delivered for service with the newly re-formed No 101 Squadron at RAF Brize Norton. When complete, the Squadron will comprise five VC10 K2s and four Super VC10 K3s. The former will carry a basic 166,000lb of fuel and the Supers 181,000lb, each supplemented by a further 28,000lb in a fuselage fuel tank. Each has three refuelling points which can be monitored by a central mounted rear-facing TV camera with a display at the flight engineer's station. Together, the advent of No 101 Squadron has increased the capacity of the tanker fleet by some 50%.

In 1984 however, there was a quantum jump in RAF in-

flight refuelling capacity when the Service's most recent transport/tanker aircraft, the Lockheed L-1011-500 Tristar also became operational at Brize Norton. Six aircraft were purchased in 1983 and were progressively converted to the tanker role by Marshalls at Cambridge. Each carries an additional 100,000lb of fuel giving a total transfer capability equal to several Victors while still carrying over 100 passengers or a comparable cargo load. Another famous numberplate has been restored in No 216 Squadron, which was formed in France on 1 April 1918. After one year as a bomber squadron flying Handley Page 0/400s it moved to Egypt and has remained a transport squadron ever since. It flew Comets from 1956 to 1975 when it

disbanded at Lyneham after several years service as the RAF's VIP squadron.

By the end of 1984, it was not impossible that the tanker fleet would be expanded by a further Tristar purchase, but as always both the costs and the manpower bill involved had to be weighed against the many other desirable items in the RAF's longer term shopping list.

In sum, the reach and flexibility of British air power had been considerably extended by the middle of the decade by new aircraft, new operational techniques and above all the considerable enlargement of the RAF's air-to-air refuelling capability. The old distinction between tactical and strategic had become blurred as aircraft designed for relatively short range operations could be projected several thousand miles across the globe in a matter of hours, no longer limited by the capacity of their own fuel tanks. A presence could be swiftly moved to a region, and equally swiftly withdrawn and redeployed; allies could be re-assured and their potential enemies reminded of the power of such a long range commitment. No military force can ever replace diplomacy as an instrument of foreign policy, but rapidly reactive long range air mobility can give it considerable support.

Above:
The first VC10 tanker to arrive at Brize Norton in 1983 to begin work-up for No 101 Squadron.

Below:
A Tornado GR1 from No 9 Squadron simulates an air-to-air refuelling approach to a potential Tristar tanker.
Crown copyright photo by A. Booth

6 Maritime Operations

When Bleriot flew the Channel in 1908, Britain could no longer depend solely on command of the sea for its security, but neither could she neglect it. Eighty years later the country still depends on seaborne trade for its continued existence; sea power remains an essential element in any defence policy. However, just as air power has grown to be an inextricable element in any campaign on land, so no conflict at sea can disregard the implications of participation from the air. So much so that command of the sea itself is no longer the sole prerogative of navies, as the Argentinian air force so emphatically reminded the world in 1982.

British maritime air power is now a potent complement of Royal Navy helicopters and Sea Harriers, generally responsible for tactical operations at sea in the close vicinity of the Fleet and under the command of an admiral, and the land-based longer range aircraft of No 18 Group, heirs to the proud traditions of Coastal Command. Group Headquarters at RAF Northwood is also the home of Commander-in-Chief Fleet and Flag Officer Submarines, thereby comprising a joint Service headquarters where surface, sub-surface and air operations can be co-ordinated with an effectiveness which was comprehensively demonstrated during the Falkland Islands campaign. Then, Adm Sir John Fieldhouse, C-in-C Fleet, was appointed Commander Task Force 317, with Air Marshal Sir John Curtiss as his Air Commander. The invaluable contribution to that conflict of the Sea Harriers and naval helicopters is well documented; it is not detailed in these pages only because our subject is the contribution of the Royal Air Force to British air power.

The largest element in RAF maritime air power is provided by four squadrons of Nimrods, now completing their modification programme from Mk 1 to Mk 2. Search and rescue duties are performed by Sea King and Wessex helicopters while two squadrons of Buccaneers provide a potent offensive arm, and the Phantoms of No 43 Squadron have a specific maritime air defence responsibility. It should however be noted that naval units operating in the eastern Atlantic, the North Sea and the Channel would be within the cover of all UK air defences whether specialised or not. Indeed, as OC 18 Group is also Air Commander Eastern Atlantic and Air Commander Channel within the NATO structure he would also assume command in war of the maritime patrol aircraft of Holland and Norway.

In peacetime, maritime security also includes fishery protection and oil rig surveillance: tasks collectively known as Off-shore Tapestry. Thus, quite apart from their considerable contribution to the Falklands war, the aircraft of No 18 Group may legitimately claim to be flying operationally regularly in peacetime also.

Maritime Reconnaissance

A primary function of No 18 Group is to provide maritime reconnaissance – the contribution of the Hawker Siddeley Nimrod MR (Maritime Reconnaissance) Mks 1 and 2. A unique aircraft in many respects, Nimrod is a derivative of the de Havilland Comet 4C airliner. Just as the Comet was the world's first jet airliner, so Nimrod is the world's first all-jet land-based maritime reconnaissance aircraft. Nimrod's four Rolls-Royce 250 Spey turbojets give it a transit cruise speed of approximately 400kt which is a considerable advantage over its piston-engine predecessors in the anti-submarine role.

The modern submarine can dive more deeply and travel more swiftly than its World War 2 ancestors and thus Nimrod's ability to reach a threatened area at high speed is very important. The anti-submarine team of surface ships, hunter-killer submarines and helicopters is closely integrated, but Nimrod's contribution in searching large areas of ocean in minimum time is unique.

The Soviet Union now has more than 300 ocean-going boats: some armed with nuclear missiles, some designed to attack allied surface fleets and some designed to hunt NATO's own submarines. To detect them Nimrod relies on a complicated blend of the human skills of a 12-man crew and advanced technology sensors. On a routine patrol from Kinloss, a Nimrod of No 120 Squadron, for example, would climb away on all four engines and transit to the search area perhaps somewhere to the northwest of the Shetlands at some 30,000ft, kept on track by the skills of the crew and an Elliot E3 inertial platform, a Decca doppler 67M and secondary Sperry GM7 Gyro Magnetic Compass system. The crew would be aware of the last known position and heading of the submarine and on reaching the search area Nimrod would descend to perhaps 6,000ft to begin a search pattern. The Captain would probably close down two engines. Thus with maximum fuel economy Nimrod, 'The Mighty Hunter', would begin to justify its sobriquet.

At this point, the quality of teamwork among the crew would become extremely important. Tactical information is co-ordinated and processed by the Elliot 920 computer but whereas some other maritime reconnaissance aircraft such as the P-3 Orion also rely on their tactical computer for analysis and decision-making, the Nimrod crew make the decisions based on computer information. Tactical information about the underwater intruder may be gleaned in several ways.

Occasionally a submarine may be caught on the surface, but such an occurrence is very rare and, as the Soviet Union builds more nuclear-powered boats, will become rarer. Nevertheless, visual look-out remains a fundamental task. The 'Autolycus' ionisation detector was able to register diesel fumes from vessels on the surface at ranges well beyond the human vision but it is those sensors which can detect the underwater enemy which are obviously the most important. A magnetic anomaly

detector (MAD) reacts to small changes in the earth's magnetic field caused by the presence of large amounts of metal. Electronic sensor equipment designed by Thomson-CSF of France is able to locate transmissions and bearings of electronic emissions. Nimrod's own radar may detect the tell-tale schnorkel of a submerged boat, but as often as not it will be located by the sonar buoys dropped in a meticulous pattern by the aircraft. Attached to each buoy, at a pre-set depth, is a microphone which through a small antenna protruding above the surface transmits the sounds in the ocean back up to the Nimrod. On the central tactical display unit the attack navigator can then see the Nimrod's own track, position of the buoys and the position and heading of the boat beneath them.

Underwater detection has been improved by the installation of the AQS-901 acoustic system which analyses and provides classification data for active and passive sonar buoys of the most modern variety either in use or under development in Britain and elsewhere in the Alliance and Commonwealth. AQS-901 displays both sonar management and acoustic data thereby enabling the operator to avoid mutual interference between sonar buoys dropped in a pattern. A large number of buoys may be monitored simultaneously and the data preserved for post-flight analysis.

Subsequent action would depend, of course, on the operating environment. In peacetime, on a routine patrol, the submarine signature, type, depth, heading and speed would be quickly logged for subsequent addition to the accumulated knowledge held by the NATO Alliance of the habits of a potential enemy.

In the Falklands War Nimrods did not encounter any Argentinian submarines. Had they done so they would have been prepared to press home attacks with a variety of air-to-surface weapons. Open press reports subsequently indicated that the Nimrod Mk 2s were cleared to deliver 1,000lb high explosive bombs, BL755 cluster bombs and the Sting Ray torpedo which was brought quickly into service ahead of the previously planned date.

Nimrod Reconnaissance

British Aerospace Nimrod MR2. The Manchester Division of British Aerospace is currently undertaking the conversion of Nimrod MR1s of the Royal Air Force into the Mk2 version – the world's most advanced maritime reconnaissance aircraft. This conversion involves the installation of Searchwater – an advanced computer assisted radar – a new acoustic processing system and a new tactical computer which increases computing speed and power by some 50 times.

Above & Above right:
Nimrod MR2 XV254 fitted with in-flight refuelling probe and carrying four AIM-9L Sidewinders. *Both BAe*

Surface Operations

Submarine hunting is not, however, Nimrod's only contribution to the maritime security of the United Kingdom. In war it could locate, track and attack enemy surface vessels and in peacetime prepares for those activities also. For example, a Nimrod of No 120 Squadron launched from Kinloss may have located the intruding submarine after less than a couple of hours of medium level search. If so, the aircraft could still have six hours endurance remaining. It might therefore be possible, depending on other training or operational demands, to exercise the crews' skills at surface searching. So, back up to transit height and then perhaps 30 minutes later and 180 miles to the southwest two engines closed again, then down through broken cloud to investigate a radar contact on the surface just outside British territorial waters. The Nimrod crews hope to discover a Soviet Navy 'Kara', 'Kotlin' or 'Udaloy', or even a humble intelligence gathering 'trawler' but they have been briefed before take-off on the last-known positions of such vessels and they know that their 'trade' is likely to be much more innocuous. From 6,000ft a small merchantman may be clearly visible, pitching and rolling in an averagely uncomfortable Eastern Atlantic.

Down to 300ft, camera hatches open, and the Nimrod sweeps over a 5,000-ton Polish coaster whose waving crew clearly see nothing sinister in the Nimrod either. Another pass, another photograph for the squadron album and, without lighting the other two engines, a steady climb and turn on to 0900 back to Kinloss. This particular sortie might be completed before dusk, but by the very nature of its environment Nimrod must be able to operate by night and day in all weathers. Identification of surface vessels at night is made possible by a powerful 70 million candle-power searchlight, the descendant of the 'Leigh' light of Bat of Biscay fame, and by an electronic flash system for night photography. The MAD, radar and sonar sensors are, of course, all applicable by night and day.

The modification of the Nimrod to Mk 2 standard has included the installation of new sensor equipment, communications and Central Tactics Display which make it the most advanced maritime patrol aircraft in the world. At the heart of the refit is the Thorn EMI Search-water primary radar used for the search, tracking and clarification of a variety of maritime targets at long range, even in adverse sea conditions, including those as small as submarine periscopes and schnorkels. Clarification is achieved dramatically by the portrayal on a television type radar screen of the actual shape and dimensions of the ship 'picked up' by the radar. Information about large numbers of simultaneous targets can be swiftly transferred to the main Tactical Display Unit which has been redesigned to cater for increased navigational precision, computing speed and display quality. The new digital computer in the system confers a 50-fold increase in capacity over that of the Nimrod Mk 1. A new communication system has been fitted and advanced electronic warfare equipment is housed in new wing pods to enhance the collection of electronic emissions.

The value of the enhanced capabilities of the Mk 2 were quickly illustrated in the Falklands campaign. Two Mk 1s from No 42 Squadron at St Mawgan arrived at Wideawake airfield on 6 April and, together with others operating from the UK and Gibraltar, provided communications links with RN patrol submarines and scanned the seas ahead of the southbound Task Force before beginning to pay particular attention to Soviet intelligence ships and submarines, whose interest the Task Force was attracting. Subsequently the Nimrod Mk 2s maintained constant surface searches of the seas between the Task Force and the Argentine mainland. We now know that the loss of the cruiser *Belgrano* had a shattering effect on the Argentinian naval leadership but at the time a surface or submarine counter-attack on Task Force 317 could never be discounted. The capability of the Mk 2s was even further enhanced at this time by their rapid acquisition of air-to-air refuelling probes: British Aerospace, Manchester Division taking only an astonishing 13 days from receiving the instructions to proceed to the first flight of a modified, restyled 'Mk P2'. Operational 24 hours clearance was complete eight days later and XV229 began operating from Wideawake four days after that. It is apparent now that the Nimrods, to provide the necessary advance warning to the Task Force and its resupply ships, flew deep into the combat range of Argentinian fighters. Wg Cdr David Emmerson, Commanding Officer of No 206 Squadron, was awarded the Air Force Cross for displaying 'courage and coolness which were a magnificent example to others'.

In addition they provided valuable co-ordination of air-to-air refuelling rendezvous between Vulcans and Victor tankers, as well as of the vital long range maritime reconnaissance missions of a specially equipped Victor to support the recapture of South Georgia early in the conflict. Several were fitted with Omega or twin Carousel Inertial Navigation Systems to enhance the navigational accuracy required for such remote and precise operations. Subsequently 16 Mk 2s were converted to P2s, all but three before the cessation of hostilities in mid-June.

Meanwhile, the Argentinians themselves were fully aware of the value of maritime reconnaissance, using a Boeing 707 of the Fuerza Aerea Argentina to shadow the

Task Force. On one occasion it was intercepted by a Nimrod Mk 2 but fortunately for the Boeing the Nimrod at that stage was unarmed. Subsequently the Nimrods were fitted with Sidewinders, but whether by accident or design, the Boeing never ventured again within range. Seldom can the flexibility of air power have been so thoroughly exemplified as by the ultimate multi-role capability of the Nimrod: originally a passenger aircraft, then a reconnaissance aircraft, bomber, communications link and then, although probably viewed askance by hardened single-seat pilots, armed as a fighter! Finally, although not having an opportunity to launch it, Nimrod was fitted with a United States – supplied air-to-surface guided missile: the Harpoon. The Defence White Paper published later in the year confirmed that 'a total of 34 Nimrods will eventually be modified to enable them to carry anti-shipping and air-to-air missiles'. Before the Falklands campaign Nimrod was already an impressive aircraft; since then it has become an extremely formidable war machine capable of far more than maritime surveillance.

Off-Shore Tapestry

Maritime air power, like other aspects, is not only available for use when open conflict has broken out. Not all the Nimrods which leave Kinloss or St Mawgan each day are training for wartime roles. Some will take off to make an immediate contribution to the security of British resources in peacetime, embarking on patrols associated with tasks known collectively in Whitehall as Off-Shore Tapestry: protection of fisheries, oilfields and rigs in the waters round the British coast. The Government decided in 1974 to begin regular surveillance of the oilrigs and associated fields, demonstrating by the presence of ships and aircraft its interest in a multi-million pound industry in which it had invested heavily. By the end of 1976, however, patrol of the oilfields became co-ordinated with fishery protection. In January 1977 the United Kingdom established a 200-mile Exclusive Economic Zone (EEZ) off the national coastline – which, where the water depth is less than 600ft, is an area of 180,000 square miles or twice that of the mainland. The Zone is divided into four patrol areas of which three are allocated to the Nimrods at Kinloss and one to those at St Mawgan. Nimrod sorties are amplified

by occasional contributions from RN Sea King helicopters.

In one of the earliest Tapestry sorties in January 1977 a Nimrod of No 120 Squadron searched 72,000 square miles, identified and classified 165 fishing boats by nationality, position, course and speed and photographed another 95 foreign vessels. On 17 May 1978 a Nimrod of No 42 Squadron from St Mawgan spotted a Spanish trawler fishing illegally, notified HM Fishery Protection Vessel *Lindisfarne*, and the Spanish skipper was subsequently fined £15,000, largely on the basis of the Nimrod crew's evidence. This was the first of several such 'airborne arrests' which in 1979 led to 24 convictions being obtained by the Ministry of Agriculture, Fisheries and Food for a variety of offences by fishing vessels within the United Kingdom's fishery zone.

The Nimrod Squadrons

Nimrod crews are trained at No 236 Maritime Operational Training Unit at RAF St Mawgan in Cornwall from where they may be posted to No 42 Squadron on the same station, or to the other end of the country to Nos 120, 201 or 206 Squadrons at Kinloss. Unlike other squadrons in No 18 Group, No 42 has not always been in the maritime business. In World War 1 it was a tactical reconnaissance squadron with the RFC in France and Italy. In World War 2 it attacked surface shipping and laid mines in the North Sea, the Mediterranean and Indian Oceans before resuming its overland traditions in Burma. In 1952, it re-formed as a maritime reconnaissance squadron flying Shackletons and served on the Beira Patrol during the blockade of Rhodesia before converting to Nimrods in 1971.

Below left:
A modern Soviet diesel 'Tango' class submarine in the South-West Approaches.

Below:
A Soviet Naval Air Force Yak-36 'Forger' on the deck of the latest Russian aircraft carrier, the *Novorssiysk*, in 1983.
Both Crown copyright photos taken by Flt Lt Stephen Smith and Crew 5 of No 42 Nimrod Squadron, St Mawgan

Above:
Buccaneers of No 12 and 208 Squadrons as detached to RAF Akrotiri in 1983, with the town of Limassol in the background. Note that the nearest Buccaneer carries an ECM pod below its starboard wing.

Right:
The British Aerospace long range anti-ship missile Sea Eagle on Buccaneer flight tests. *BAe*

Three-quarters of the Nimrod force is, however, based at Kinloss within easy reach of the critical waters of the Eastern Atlantic and the Iceland–Faroes Gap. No 120 squadron was formed near the end of World War 1 only, but between 1941 and 1945, flying Liberators from Ireland and Iceland, sank 19 U-boats and damaged many others. After 20 years flying Shackletons it also re-equipped with Nimrods in 1971. No 201 Squadron, on the other hand, was originally No 1 Squadron of the Royal Naval Air Service and, like the other RNAS squadrons, was absorbed into the Royal Air Force in April 1918 with the addition of 200 to its original squadron number. Since then, with only occasional breaks in service, it has specialised in maritime activities. It flew anti-surface and anti-submarine patrols in World War 2 and swept the Channel prior to the Normandy landings. In 1948 it contributed to the Berlin Airlift, flying its Sunderlands on to Lake Havel, and with No 230 Squadron was the last RAF squadron to fly the four-engined flying boat at Pembroke Dock until February 1957. After 13 years with Shackletons it became the first RAF Nimrod squadron in October 1970. The third Nimrod squadron at Kinloss, No 206, also has RNAS roots being renumbered from RNAS No 6 in April 1918 while still a heavy bomber squadron operating in France. Since 1936 it has flown almost entirely in maritime roles. Equipped with Ansons, Hudsons, Fortresses and Liberators during World War 2 it operated off the German, Norwegian and Danish coasts as well as out over the Atlantic. During a short spell with Transport Command after the war, it also flew on the Berlin Airlift before reassuming its maritime role with Shackletons at St Eval in 1952. It re-equipped with the Nimrod at Kinloss one month after No 201 Squadron in November 1970.

Anti-Surface Shipping Operations

The Nimrod's newly-acquired anti-surface shipping potential is a valuable supplement to that of the 'custom built' Buccaneers of Nos 12 and 208 Squadrons, and of No 227 Operational Conversion Unit at RAF Lossiemouth.

No 12 Squadron has been a bomber squadron since its formation at Newhaven in 1915, flying Wellingtons and Lancasters in World War 2 and Vulcans during the zenith of the V-Force between 1962 and 1967. In 1940, Flg Off Garland and Sgt Gray won the first Victoria Crosses in the Royal Air Force in World War 2 when they led a low level formation attack against the heavily defended Vroenhoeven bridge over the Albert Canal in Belgium. They were both killed when their Fairey Battle was shot down but the attack was pressed home successfully. In 1969 No 12 Squadron re-formed at Honington with Buccaneers and since then, being assigned to SACLANT, spends most of its training in a maritime environment.

No 208 Squadron was formed on 1 April 1918 at Teteghem, near Dunkirk, from No 8 Squadron RNAS. From 1919 it saw almost unbroken tactical offensive or reconnaissance support service in the Mediterranean or Middle East until its disbandment after flying Hunters at Bahrein in 1971. In 1974 the Squadron re-formed at Honington with Buccaneers, moving to Lossiemouth in 1982.

Aircrew for both squadrons are converted at Lossiemouth on No 237 OCU, whose aircraft can quickly supplement the squadrons in their operational commitments. The Buccaneers were also deployed for several years in RAF Germany in their overland role but now concentrate on the mission for which they were originally designed by the Blackburn Aircraft Co: anti-surface shipping strikes. Their two Rolls-Royce Spey engines develop over 22,000lb thrust and give them extended low level range which can be further extended by 'buddy-buddy' air-to-air refuelling. In their large, traditional

bomb bay they can carry free-fall conventional or nuclear weapons, while on their wing pylons they carry rockets or the Martel TV-guided stand-off anti-radar missile. A typical attack profile was flown during an exercise on detachment to the US Naval Air Station at Key West, Florida in March 1983. The crews, from No 12 Squadron, flew in formations of six aircraft at 100ft above the sea to deliver the TV-guided version of Martel, but they also train to attack in singletons or other combinations.

Also in 1983 the rapid mobility and long range of the Buccaneers were demonstrated in more serious circumstances. In spring a detachment deployed to the South Atlantic where extended range exercises were flown from RAF Stanley supported by the Hercules tankers of No 1312 Flight. Then, when the Lebanese crisis arose later in the year, six Buccaneers drawn from both Nos 12 and 208 Squadrons were flown to Akrotiri in Cyprus to provide offensive support, had that become necessary, to the British contingent in Beirut. On this occasion, because of the close proximity of civilian areas to potential military targets, they carried laser-guided bombs to ensure absolute precision and ECM pods for use against possible ground-to-air defences. Happily they were not called upon to use

their weapons, but British television recorded at least one extremely low level visit through the city of Beirut rather than over it, to demonstrate most dramatically what they could have done if required. It was indeed a well-nigh perfect example of the way in which the potential of air power could be used to emphasise interest, and determination, in a troubled international area.

The defensive capability of the Buccaneer has been enhanced by the carriage of Sidewinders but its offensive strength is being considerably increased with the acquisition of the British Aerospace Sea Eagle missile. Sea Eagle has been reported to have a range well in excess of 60 miles, to have high resistance to electronic countermeasures and to carry a large warhead weighing approximately 500lb. It is optimised for attack against a ship's hull with a head shaped to ensure penetration even at shallow contact angles. It is claimed to possess very high target discrimination with an ability to recognise a target by radar profile and position. It is known to be a considerably more effective weapon than the Exocets used so devastatingly by the Super Etendards in the South Atlantic, and will ensure that the Buccaneer remains a very powerful maritime attack force for at least another decade.

The new Range Safety and Target Towing Launch for No 10 Port Squadron Royal Corps of Transport based at Royal Air Force Akrotiri practising its role as part of the Air-Sea Rescue Service co-ordinated from Episkopi and run in conjunction with a Search and Rescue helicopter of No 84 Squadron.

Search and Rescue

For several years the Nimrod force has maintained one aircraft at one hour readiness for search and rescue (SAR) duties within the United Kingdom SAR Region which extends 1,000 miles out into the Atlantic. The Nimrod's speed, range and sensor equipment make it ideally suited to the initial crucial tasks of locating the incident and co-ordinating rescue ships and helicopters. In September 1978, for example, the crew of a ditched RNAF Atlantique was rescued by Sea King helicopters within one hour of being located by the SAR Nimrod scrambled from Kinloss. Ironically, nine members of the crew of a second Dutch Atlantique were rescued from the sea in similar manner in February 1981 when this time a Nimrod from No 42 Squadron co-ordinated the helicopter rescue.

Not all mercy missions are so successful. In September 1982 a Bell 212 helicopter en route to the northern North Sea oilfields crashed into the sea in the early hours of a stormy night with bad visibility. Sadly, there were no survivors of the crash but the Searchwater-equipped SAR Nimrod demonstrated its ability for seven hours to control eight search helicopters and a stream of routine airfield air traffic, while relaying information and search updates to surface shipping also in the area.

But, naturally enough, the bulk of the actual rescues are made by the helicopters of Nos 202 and 22 Squadrons, dispersed at eight stations round the United Kingdom. Established primarily to rescue downed aircrew, both RAF and RN helicopters spend far more of their time helping yachtsmen, swimmers, climbers and other civilians in distress. Successes can be spectacular but occasionally tragedy strikes, as when a winchman from No 202 Squadron Detachment at Coltishall was killed in 1980 while trying to resuce the pilot of a USAF A-10 in the North Sea.

No 202 Squadron re-equipped in 1978 with the twin-jet Westland Sea King HAS Mk3, which is fitted with advanced all-weather search and navigation equipment enhanced by auto-pilot and on-board computer. In theory it can carry 15 survivors in addition to its four crew members over a radius of action of about 270 miles. This alone would have marked a major increase in capacity over the previous well-tried Wessex and Whirlwinds, but on 2 October 1980 another No 202 Squadron Sea King,

Above:
A long way from home: a Sea King of No 202 Squadron from Coltishall on standby at Port Stanley. *Author*

Above:
A Wessex Mk 2 of No 84 Squadron with its British Forces Lebanon Union Jack. *D. Calvert*

this time from Lossiemouth, demonstrated what the aircraft could do in the hands of a determined, skilful and brave crew. In an operation lasting more than 3½ hours and despite 70ft high seas, gale force winds, flames and toxic fumes, Flt Lt Michael Lakey and his crew rescued 22 survivors from the burning Swedish chemical cargo ship *Finneagle* 50 miles off the Orkneys. Not surprisingly the crew received one George Medal, one AFC, one Air Force Medal, one Queen's Commendation for valuable service in the air and one Queen's Commendation for brave conduct as well as many other awards from different sources. This rescue was, however, only a dramatic example of the long traditions of both helicopter squadrons.

No 202 Squadron, originally RNAS No 2, flew fixed-wing aircraft in a variety of maritime roles until 1964 when it took over the number of No 228 SAR Whirlwind Squadron at Leconfield which itself had inherited No 275's Sycamores in 1959. It is now deployed at Lossiemouth, Boulmer, Leconfield and Port Stanley. No 22 Squadron also originated in World War I and discharged fighter, reconnaissance and training duties before becoming a specialist maritime squadron in 1934. Since 1955 No 22 has flown SAR helicopters and in 1980 was deployed in flights of Whirlwinds and Wessex at Leuchars, Chivenor, Valley and Coltishall.

In November 1982 Master Air Loadmaster Bob Danes, then based with the Wessex detachment at Coltishall, earned the rare distinction of a bar to his AFC when he was lowered to the deck of a Chinese vessel in the North Sea to help transfer two seriously ill seamen to hospital. Despite dense spray and a 60kt wind the winchman was lowered on to the pitching deck awash with 50ft waves where, having applied first aid, 'with great risk to his own life and little assistance he manoeuvred the stretcher back to the winching area where both he and the casualty were recovered to the aircraft. Undaunted he then repeated the operation and successfully recovered a second casualty to the aircraft'. Not surprisingly, the pilot of the Wessex who held his aircraft steady in such conditions, Flt Lt Alan Coy, was awarded the Queen's Commendation for valuable service in the air.

These are but dramatic examples of challenges which the crews of the SAR squadrons can expect to be called upon to meet every day, facing an enemy in the elements which demands personal and professional qualities comparable to those required in actual combat itself. This is maritime air power in miniature: the protection and rescue of individuals. From there it spans the spectrum from supporting forces on land, to patrolling the Falklands Islands, to shadowing surface vessels, to identifying errant fishermen and, should deterrence ever fail, to hunting and destroying enemy vessels on and below the surface of the oceans. With the submarines, surface vessels and tactical aircraft of the Royal Navy, the aircraft of No 18 Group protect the ocean flanks of the United Kingdom.

7 Air Power, Manpower and Resources

Since its earliest days air power has called for its implementation on men with special skills and character, and on resources frequently at the forefront of technological development. By the middle of the 1980s the demands were as insistent, but manpower and resources were becoming increasingly expensive. Many of the world's leading air forces were engaged in studies on how to continue to implement one of Lord Trenchard's best known dicta: 'Remember that the one great thing to which you should at all times apply your thoughts and brains is the expansion of the power of material and personnel without increasing either. That way lies economy'. Now however an old question was being re-examined. What was the future of the manned aircraft in an era of increased computerisation, increasingly sophisticated surface-to-air defences, automated satellite reconnaissance activity and the apparently inevitably increasing unit costs of each aircraft and each item of supporting

Below:
A satellite at one end, and a hand-held Satcom terminal at the other. Longer term implications?

equipment? On the ground, how far would automatic data processing and the availability of replacement parts manufactured simply to be exchanged for unserviceable items reduce the need for many different kinds of tradesmen? There were several different answers to each part of each question, and by no means all the answers were devoid of self interest on the part of those offering them, but it was possible to speculate generally on where some of the answers might best be sought.

For example, one school of thought argued that if one could confidently and accurately predict the location of a target at a given time, and if there was no possible likelihood of it being able to evade an attack by moving, then it might not be necessary to either overfly that target or even approach close to it to attack, if there were other more cost effective means available. Consequently, in the United States, projects were underway to develop either ground or air-launched missiles which could reach, locate and destroy such targets either with a primary warhead or with inert or guided sub-munitions. Runways and command centres for example were prime candidates for such attack. Considerable technical problems remained and, perhaps in a potentially tense political situation in war, so too did problems of missile identification amenable to arms control negotiations. Yet the philosophy underlying the research was not new; it had after all prompted the development of both inter-continental and intermediate range missiles a generation earlier to take over the traditional, strategic role of the manned bomber against an enemy's industrial centres. The transfer of the British deterrent responsibility from the V-Force to the Royal Navy's Polaris missiles was Britain's response to those circumstances and in 1984 it was unlikely that longer term thinking in London was far removed from that in Washington, which was now extending such ideas to the combat theatre. Tornado itself could in theory become a long range missile launcher for use against a wider range of targets.

If, on the other hand, timely intelligence was required, satellites were already providing real time pictorial and electronic reconnaissance while a country with the inclination and money to spend could purchase any one of several drone systems to provide tactical information from the immediate area of the combat zone. By 1984 there were many detailed accounts of the use by Israel of 'spies in the sky' over combat regions such as that in the Bekaa Valley in the Lebanon. But as recent tests by both super-powers have demonstrated, a satellite may become as vulnerable to physical destruction as it is at present to jamming. The offensive-defensive pendulum will swing just as regularly in electronic warfare as it has traditionally done in all other kinds of warfare. As long as a country has a technological lead and dependable intelligence about potentially hostile equipment, it may confidently rely on

Above:
University of London Chancellor's Parade May 82. HRH Princess Anne (Chancellor of the University of London) inspecting a Guard of Honour provided by the University of London Air Squadron. With HRH, Wg Cdr K. W. Jarvis (OC ULAS) and APO A. S. Rycroft (Guard Commander).

Right:
'Manpower' is an all-embracing term. A ground branch officer candidate at Biggin Hill. *Crown copyright photo by SACW Diane Edmonds*

automated systems. If however its confidence is misplaced, it may fall victim to electronic surprise, such as that met by the Israeli Air Force in 1973 when it flew against the Egyptian SAM-6 batteries. Whatever else may be predicted confidently about any future air war in Central Europe, it is that it will be enshrouded in electronic attack and defence. Arguably, such circumstances are not the most ideal in which to let success or failure depend on the reliability of automated equipment.

But even if it were to become possible to rely confidently on automated systems for reconnaissance and some form of attack, so much else in the contribution of air power in peace and war could, well into the forseeable future, only be carried out by a combination of man and machine. Conventional attacks on highly mobile systems such as armoured formations for example will continue to present difficulties to preplanned inflexible attack, as will reconnaissance in areas where the enemy presence is uncertain

or out of range of tactical drones. Air mobility as a whole will continue to require swiftly responding aeroplanes and helicopters. Reliance solely on surface-to-air missiles for air defence not only induces vulnerability to various kinds of countermeasures, but also to saturation in the face of hostile concentration: a particularly critical weakness in any circumstances where an enemy could be expected to have the initiative in time, place and method of attack. Indeed, this one example epitomises the continued caution required when postulating circumstances in which the manned aircraft can confidently be discounted. Aircraft can evade swiftly, especially aircraft with a short runway requirement like Harrier or Tornado; they can respond swiftly; and above all they can be redirected quickly to effect their own concentration in attack or defence. And, as has already been illustrated in earlier chapters, they can be modified to perform roles never thought of by their original designers. But discounting is only one error; the other is forgetting: forgetting that the most important contribution to a nation's defence which armed services can ever provide is to make their own actual use in combat unnecessary. The manned aircraft has ready and widely projectable visibility.

It may well be, therefore, that the future of the manned aircraft lies in the correct answer to a slightly different question: what, given the likely directions of the development of aircraft and weapon technologies, is the most cost-effective combination of man and machine in the whole range of air power functions already described? In Britain, lacking the population and economic wealth of the super-powers, and with alternative priorities from public expenditure always facing governments – whatever their political line – it is essential that the balance between air power, manpower and resources is finely struck.

Above right:
Briefing cadets on the Sedbergh glider cockpit.

Right:
Sort it out Bloggs! Preparing to taxi at Bristol University Air Squadron.

Below:
A Chipmunk of No 7 Air Experience Flight, RAF Newton, overflies Trent Bridge, home of Nottingham CCC. *Air Clues*

Manpower

In the RAF, the expression manpower also encompasses the 5,000 members of the Women's Royal Air Force who, although not yet considered for pilot and navigator training, compete on equal terms with their male colleagues for appointment and promotion in every branch and trade in which they serve. In 1984 members of the WRAF also began to take their place alongside servicemen in the South Atlantic as appropriate domestic arrangements became available. The degree of professional skill and personal qualities demanded not just in the Atlantic, but for RAF commitments worldwide, are not however produced in a matter of hours, or even weeks. They are the product of a training system which has been emulated by many other air forces and which continues every day, in one form or another, to ensure the instant readiness of the RAF's front line aircraft.

In the 1920s the government of the day declared that defence policy could assume that the country would not enter a major war for at least 10 years, an assumption known familiarly as The 10 Year Rule. At the same time an aircraft company could design and build a warplane in little more than a year. Then, the Air Staff could expect 10 years notice of war, and new equipment in less than a year. In the 1980s they have to prepare to fight a war which could be forced upon them with far less than a year's notice yet re-equipment programmes can take up to 10 years from concept to operation. That preparedness begins with the training, maintenance and other units of Royal Air Force Support Command, whose function is succinctly explained in the inscription in its crest: "That Eagles May Fly".

In fact, RAF Support Command takes a keen interest in air-minded young men well before they reach an age to consider joining the Service. In 1984 the Air Training Corps had a membership of some 40,000 probationer and enrolled cadets in 42 wings, 899 squadrons and 112 detached flights spread across the UK. Within the aegis of the Commander-in-Chief of Support Command fall the 50 Chipmunks, Huskies and Bulldogs flown by the 13 air experience flights and the 27 gliding schools of the ATC.

Above left:
HM Queen Elizabeth the Queen Mother meets instructors of the Central Flying School.

Left:
'You have it Bloggs'. A Jet Provost begins a starboard break.

Below left:
Dominie T1s from No 6 FTS, Finningley on a training detachment to Gibraltar.

Above:
Not often seen out on its own; a single Red Arrow finishing off the bomb-burst at low level.

Here young cadets can get their first taste of flying in addition to discovering some of the basic intricacies of associated ground trade responsibilities in their training classrooms. Indeed in recent years a quarter of all RAF officer and airmen entrants, and a third of the apprentice intake, have had previous ATC experience. Some cadets may move from school to university or polytechnic, and there they have an opportunity to take their air-mindedness a stage further by joining a University Air Squadron.

The University Air Squadrons
In 1925 Lord Trenchard instituted the first University Air Squadron at Cambridge. By 1984 there were 16 squadrons in the United Kingdom associated with 36 universities, 29 colleges and 11 polytechnics. They provide a military focus and unit for all RAF university cadet officers and flying training for those entering the general duties branch. In addition, the squadrons include Volunteer Reserve members who will also be trained to fly but who do not necessarily have a commitment to join the Service. Squadrons are staffed by regular RAF officers, all qualified flying instructors (QFIs), and the squadron training programme includes groundschool training at squadron headquarters, flying training at a nearby civilian or military airfield, and summer camps at operational RAF stations.

The undergraduate pilot is expected to fit his flying into his academic curriculum without detriment to either. Each month he is called upon to fly an 'essential exercise' check to demonstrate that he can safely complete those exercises which he has covered to date. After he has gone solo he is accompanied by his QFI only to check his competence. For example, a Royal Air Force VR undergraduate with 18 months experience on the Queen's University Air Squadron at Belfast with 40 hours dual and 10 hours solo on the Bulldog could expect to do an 'essential exercise' check which would include spinning, aerobatics, stalling and a practice force-landing pattern in the local flying area of the Newtownards Peninsula south of Belfast Lough.

The detail of this type of sortie begins in the squadron operations room with the met briefing by the chief instructor and the flight briefing by the student's own QFI. Then, out on to the tarmac – probably chilled by the perennial fresh breeze from the adjacent Belfast Lough – to the pre-flight check on the Bulldog. The Scottish Aviation T Mk 1 Bulldog entered service with the Central Flying School in July 1973 and is now flown by the University Air squadrons and the Royal Naval Elementary Flying Training Squadrons at Leeming. It is small enough for the undergraduate to inspect thoroughly without stretching too far: 33ft wingspan, 23ft long and almost 9ft high. It is powered by a single 200 hp Avco-Lycoming 10-360-A1B6 engine which gives a maximum range of 400 miles at a cruising speed of 120kt. It is a conventional side-by-side basic trainer, stable and tolerant in the air and with a comfortable landing speed of 65mph.

After completing the external, pre-start and pre-take-off checks this student is ready for clearance to join the airspace near Belfast. At 60kt the Bulldog is airborne and climbs at 80kt to 2,000ft to stay below Aldergrove control area. On this flight, as on all UAS flights, the student pilot must keep a sharp lookout, not only for scheduled passenger aircraft leaving or descending towards the local airport but also for light civilian aircraft buzzing, sometimes a little unconcernedly, from nearby airfields such as Newtownards. Fortunately, however, all UAS have access to low-flying areas where such hazards are not so common. The pilot from Queens would turn south towards Donaghadee and begin to climb to about 7,000ft to begin his first exercise: the controlled spin.

The student, who throughout the flying training organisation is affectionately referred to as 'Bloggs', completes his HASELL checks (height, airframe, security, engine, location and lookout), rolling out of his 'lookout' turn two miles south of Donaghadee. Then the familiar sequence: maintain height, keep aircraft in balance and then at 60kt apply full rudder, control column fully back; up and over and slowly – hopefully – settling into a gentle spin. After three full turns he'll check that the throttle is closed, the direction of the spin from the turn needle, apply full opposite rudder, push the stick fully forward until the spin stops, centralise control and ease out of the dive.

Before 'Bloggs' completes the remainder of his exercise programme he is highly likely to experience a sudden silence, induced by his QFI to simulate engine failure. This demands a no-warning practice force-landing pattern, and over the small fields, rolling hills and stone-walled country lanes of Northern Ireland, suitable landing areas are not easy to spot. Nevertheless, the field is chosen, and a pattern flown to lead to an overshoot at 150ft rather than the actual touch-down. Subsequently, return to the airfield at Sydenham by the side of the Lough is accompanied by simulated radio failure and possibly even a further engine 'seizure'.

The exercise at Belfast resembles those flown every month at all the University Air Squadrons as students work towards qualification for the Preliminary Flying Badge, usually after about 85 hours. Although only a small percentage of the VR students will actually join the RAF, all will learn a great deal about flying, about the RAF and about its contribution to the national defence. Those who do join the Service will not be taken by surprise by the exceptionally high standard set and demanded by the formal Flying Training Schools (FTS).

The Flying Training Schools

The standards of flying training demanded at both University Air Squadrons and Flying Training Schools are set at one of the oldest and most prestigious units in military aviation history. The Central Flying School (CFS), with its headquarters at RAF Leeming, was formed at Upavon in 1912 and since then has trained the QFIs not only of the RAF, Royal Navy and Army but of 54 Commonwealth and foreign air forces. The function of CFS is quite specific, 'To train flying instructors, on both fixed and rotary wing aircraft who, by their skill, knowledge and enthusiasm, will help to maintain the flying efficiency of the RAF at the highest level.' Fixed-wing students complete some 85 hours flying instruction in 25 weeks while potential helicopter instructors complete 70 hours in 13 weeks. Fast jet training on the Hawk is carried out at RAF Valley and helicopter flying takes place at RAF Shawbury on the Gazelle.

Nor does an instructor's development finish when he graduates from CFS. He will be awarded a B-2 or exceptionally a B-1 instructor category, but at least once a year thereafter he will be examined and recategorised by members of the Examining Wing of CFS. The Wing, a

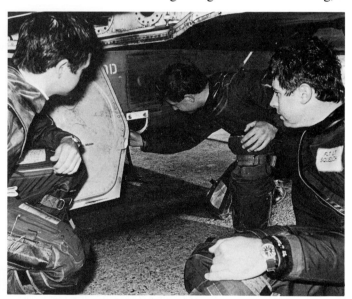

Tactical Weapons Unit

'As long as the RAF continues with such comprehensive TWU training, I've no doubt RAF fighter pilots will continue their world-renowned tradition of excellence in tactical aviation.'

Left:
Students receiving instructions in pre-flight planning prior to a navigation sortie.

Above:
Pre-flight checks on an aircraft's gun before a gun-firing sortie.

Right:
A Weapons Instructor marking the target flag after it has been used in an air-to-air gun firing practice.

component of CFS since 1927, ensures that instructional methods throughout the flying training organisation remain at the highest standard and that new ideas and techniques are co-ordinated and disseminated.

CFS also administers and supervises what the Royal Air Force unequivocally assumes to be the most accomplished aerobatic team in the world: the nine members of the Red Arrows. They epitomise the discipline, skill, teamwork and sheer professionalism which has been the pride of the Royal Air Force since its earliest days and which permeates all squadrons whether regularly in the public eye or not.

After graduating from CFS the majority of instructors will be posted to one of the FTS or UAS administered by RAF Support Command. Now all initial officer training is carried out at the RAF College. Thereafter, direct entrant would-be pilots without the requisite previous flying experience undergo 15 hours flying on the Chipmunk at the Flying Selection Squadron to select those with suitable aptitude to start basic flying training. Direct entrants with the requisite previous flying experience and those who pass the flying selection start the basic flying training course on the Jet Provost 3A at either Linton-on-Ouse or Church Fenton, or on the Jet Provost 5A at Cranwell. The basic phase of the direct entry basic flying training course comprises 93 hours flying and lasts 37 weeks.

The British Aerospace Jet Provost T3A entered service with the RAF in 1959. Powered by a Rolls-Royce Viper Mk 102 turbojet producing 1,750lb static thrust, it is unpressurised, has a maximum level flight speed of 326mph and a range of 565 miles. The more powerful T5A has a pressurised cockpit, modified airframe, maximum level flight speed of 440 mph and a range of 900 miles.

Entrants from the University Air Squadrons will normally have completed 95 hours on the Bulldog and will stay at Cranwell to fly a further 75 on the JP5A on the graduate entrant basic flying training course. Their basic phase lasts 31 weeks.

On completion of the basic phase, all pilots are streamed according to their aptitudes, the needs of the Service and, where possible, personal inclinations, to fast jet, multi-engine or helicopter aircraft. In view of the front-line configuration of the RAF, the great majority of pilots will embark on the route which will ultimately lead to Harrier, Jaguar, Phantom, Buccaneer or Tornado. They will first complete 58 hours on the JP5A at Cranwell, then move to No 4 FTS at Valley to begin 75 advanced flying hours on the British Aerospace (Hawker Siddeley) Hawk T1. Powered by a single Rolls-Royce/Turbomeca RT172.06.11 Adour 851 turbofan engine, Hawk has a maximum level flight speed of 540kt and a range of 690 miles. Stressed to +8 and −4g, Hawk was designed to be fully aerobatic but it is also simpler to understand and easier to fly in the elementary stages than its predecessor, the Folland Gnat. Consequently it has quickly achieved considerable popularity with students and instructors alike and conversion

times have been cut, thereby leaving more syllabus hours for applied exercises such as low-flying navigation or formation. Training can therefore be more heavily weighted towards the skills essential to a later operational environment. Its increased range permits a student to fly more complex series of exercises which allow him to experience a longer and heavier cockpit workload than was possible on the Gnat. Moreover, the aircraft was designed from the outset as an advanced trainer; it is of rugged construction and has a long fatigue life which should ensure that it continues into service well into the 1990s. In that period it can be readily modified to carry more advanced avionic equipment such as a simple head-up display or offset TACAN by which to simulate INAS operation. Thereby, the gap between advanced flying training and conversion to the next generation of fast jet operational aircraft will be reduced still further.

If, on the other hand, the student pilot has been selected for the Nimrod, Hercules, VC10, Tristar or Victor fleets, his development pattern will differ appropriately. After completing his basic phase he will spend another 27 hours lead-in training on the JP3A or 5A before going to Finningley, the RAF's centre for multi-engine and multi-crew training. There he will remain for 20 weeks, during which he spends six weeks in ground school learning about the Jetstream, meteorology, flight planning and aircrew survival. He spends 45 hours in the air and up to another 45 in the flight simulator. He will also begin to learn that he is not only to be responsible for an airframe and a mission. Although not having the high speed low-level demands of his colleagues at Valley, he becomes aware of the responsibilities of captaincy: leadership within an aircraft, as opposed to leadership of other crews in other aircraft.

The British Aerospace (Scottish Aviation) Jetstream T Mk 1 has been in service with the RAF from November 1976. It is used by the Multi-Engine Training Squadron at RAF Finningley, both to train student pilots in the multi-engined role and to provide refresher training for RAF pilots who are returning to operational roles.

The RAF Jetstream is powered by two Turbomeca

Above:
A Hawk T Mk 1A of No 151 Squadron from RAF Chivenor Tactical Weapons Unit.

Below:
Female aircrew of the future? Visit by girls from the local Air Venture Corps to RAF Honington.

112

Astazou 16 turboprops which each provide 985ehp for take-off. The fully-pressurised aircraft provides flight deck seating for instructor and student pilots with a third seat for an additional crew member. The fuselage provides for up to four additional passengers. The flight deck is equipped with a comprehensive range of VHF and UHF communications, navigation instrumentation and modern flight instrumentation which includes the Sperry Stars Flight Director System. It has a cruising speed of 215kt and a range of up to 1,200nm.

Helicopter Training

The third group of pilots to be streamed in the later stages of their flying training will go to the helicopter force. Unlike their colleagues staying in the fixed wing environment, they will leave the JP3A or 5A on completion of their basic phase and move to No 2 FTS at Shawbury. There they will spend 28 weeks flying the Gazelle and Wessex helicopters before, like their fixed wing contemporaries, they are awarded their wings on successful completion of their advanced flying stage. They fly 76 hours on the Anglo-French Gazelle HT MR 3 which, although light and small, has a cruising speed of 140mph and a range of some 400 miles, followed by a futher 50 hours on the heavier Westland Wessex Mk 60. The search and rescue element of the training will be carried out at Valley, where Snowdonia and the Irish Sea provide training areas which frequently call for full operational sorties. Although the new pilots will all graduate to one of the helicopter OCUs, they will not necessarily spend the whole of their flying careers on rotary wing aircraft, any more than their fixed wing colleagues will remain on one type. And, unless they fly only Harriers or Jaguars, they will sooner or later learn to fly as a team with navigators, who have their own training pattern after completion of initial officer training.

Navigator Training

The role of the navigator in the RAF changed a great deal between 1960 and 1985 and the demands upon him in the next decade are unlikely to decrease. In all aircraft his equipment has become more sophisticated which on the

'Red Flag 83'

The 'Red Flag' exercise area in the Nevada desert is designed to simulate war conditions so that pilots training there gain 'combat experience'. Because of the excellence of the range, RAF squadrons have taken part in 'Red Flag' exerices since 1977.

Above:
Buccaneers at Nellis AFB, with a No 16 Squadron aircraft in the foreground.

Below:
No 54 Squadron Jaguars returning to Nellis AFB after a 'Red Flag' sortie. *Crown copyright photo by SAC Chris Rowley*

Bottom:
A US Navy Intruder slips past a No XV Squadron Buccaneer. *Crown copyright photo by SAC Chris Rowley*

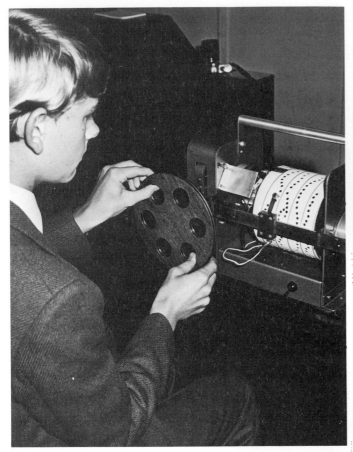

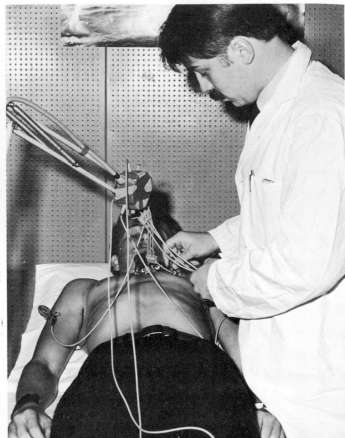

one hand has reduced some of the time traditionally allocated to the 'mechanical' aspect of calculation and plotting, but at the same time has called for swifter reactions and greater co-ordination and analysis of information. But of greater significance have been the challenges posed by high speed low level flight: regularly in the Buccaneer, Phantom, Vulcan and Canberra and frequently in the Nimrod. The challenge has been heightened dramatically as the Tornado GR1 assumes its multi-role operations, while the F2 will maintain the demand for the interceptor navigators, and the transport and helicopter forces will continue to require operational skills worldwide.

Consequently, as navigation training at Finningley entered the 1980s it was modified to prepare most effectively for what would be a considerable variety of tasks. Whereas previously aspiring navigators spent 16 weeks on Bulldogs and 'academics', 26 weeks (77 hours) on the British Aerospace Dominie T1 and six weeks (15 hours) on the JP3A before streaming for advanced low or high level training, now the basic phase has been reduced to 29 weeks (44 hours Dominie and 20 hours Jet Provost) followed by a more role-orientated advanced phase of 22 weeks which allows for stream switching if required when a student's provisional posting is known. In all phases of the course extensive use is made of the Dominie ground simulator.

Airborne exercises may start at 35.000ft at a little over 200kt. While radar is the navigator's primary positional aid, he must learn all the traditional techniques and gradually learn to deal with the pressures and procedures of crowded airways and unscheduled diversions. Later he will fly at 1,000ft in the jet Provost, learning mental dead-reckoning techniques using only topographical maps and

a stopwatch. Gradually, he will fly lower, until at 250ft his tasks will be inceased to include radio calls, look-out and fuel management in addition to his navigation. In the advanced phases, role specialisation will determine whether the student increases his low level reactions and responsibilities or concentrates on the complexities of astro-navigation, limited aids and airways restrictions.

For the air defence student there will be an introduction to methods of air interception and combat flying; for those due to join the Tornado or Buccaneer forces it will be the first insight into low level target attacks and associated route planning and checking. In a very few months one

Aircrew Selection

Far left:
It looks so simple: aircrew aptitude testing at Biggin Hill.

Above left:
An ECG test for an aircrew candidate at Biggin Hill.

Above:
Practical ingenuity, initiative and leadership tests for would-be aircrew at Biggin Hill.

Left:
. . . and finally! Will he make a pilot or won't he? The Aircrew Selection Board at Biggin Hill, led by the Commandant, decides the future of an applicant.
All Crown copyright photos by SACW Diane Edmonds

might find himself at night at 600ft 500 miles out over the Atlantic, another slipping into a narrow Himalayan valley, another negotiating crowded airways off the eastern seaboard of the United States and another following the contours of a Scottish snowscape at 400kt: and all can expect the same question – 'Where are we, nav?' In Tornado he may be given much more technical assistance, but he has much less time in which to apply it.

Meanwhile, all three variants of Nimrod, the Hercules, the Victors, Tristars and VC10s will continue to need additional crew members: the air engineers, air electronics operators and other specialists. These also will continue to be trained at Finningley before moving on to the precise crew skill training at the operational conversion units, such as those at St Mawgan or Lyneham.

The Tactical Weapons Unit
Those pilots who are going to join the Harrier, Jaguar, Buccaneer or Tornado squadrons begin their transition from flying training to combat training at a Tactical Weapons Unit (TWU) where they will be introduced to the special skills of combat tactics and weapon delivery. As at Valley they will fly the Hawk T1, thereby removing any need at this stage for further conversion to a different aircraft. It was pleasing to read in the June 1983 edition of the American *Air Force Magazine* a very complimentary account of TWU training at Chivenor by a USAF officer on exchange duties with the RAF. His professional analysis included the following observations:

'*The Programme*
At the TWU, these fledgling fighter pilots and "fighter-gators" are exposed to tactical thinking in depth before becoming part of the "real air force." The course is not academically oriented, but is flying intensive. My impression is that the ultimate goal is to make flying second nature – just like riding a bicycle.

'As previously mentioned, the main course is designed around the student pilot. It takes approximately four months to complete and involves about sixty sorties actually flown by the student pilot. Currently, there is no formal syllabus for a nav student, but he's expected to fly a minimum of twenty-five hours (about twenty-five sorties). Nav students always fly with an instructor pilot and, preferable, fly a few different sorties in each phase.

'Most flying in the Hawk is done at speeds of 420 knots or greater; operating at such speeds is typical of most line fighters. Several phases are used to enhance further essential skills and to build confidence. Starting with a brief three-sortie familiarization phase to acquaint the student with TWU operations, these phases follow a building-block approach. Subsequent phases include formation low-level navigation, weapons, air combat maneuvering, and simulated attack profiles. I was very impressed with the amount and type of training these aviators receive at such an early stage in their careers.

'Five sorties make up the formation phase. From takeoff to landing, tactical formations are emphasized heavily on each mission. First, students receive training at medium level, then progressively lower to 500 feet above the ground. These tactical formations are essentially the same as those used throughout the RAF fighter force. Both pilots and navs learn formation terminology, geometry, and maneuver. They will continue to build on formation skills in other phases. Eventually, in the low-level phase, the student pilot will participate in tactical formations with up to four aircraft, and he must be able to maneuver safely and efficiently as an integral part of the formation.'

'In the weapons phase, students are introduced to basic weaponry concepts; the optical weapon aiming sight (gunsight), an essential tool of all fighter aircraft, is given particular emphasis . . . Next is the air combat maneuvering phase. To be effective in the air-to-air arena, a fighter pilot must know the basics of fighting alone vs another aircraft (1 v 1) or fighting with a wingman vs another aircraft (2 v 1). In teaching these basics, the TWU excels'.

'Success in the phase is determined by a student's ability to integrate a multitude of planning factors into the mission. For a given target these factors include determining the right weapon and delivery parameters to achieve the desired level of destruction against a given target, selecting the correct attack axis for optimum weapon effectiveness, locating a dominant feature along the preferred attack track to serve as a visual initial point (IP) for the final target run, developing a route to the IP which avoids simulated enemy defenses, and, finally,

planning defensive reactions against potential enemy interceptors and enemy surface defenses.

'After the mission is planned, it's time to fly the plan. Mission execution at 250 feet using only heading, airspeed, map, and stopwatch is difficult enough, but throw in a "bounce" and at times the task seems impossible. The bounce is another Hawk flown by an instructor pilot simulating an enemy interceptor. His mission is to disrupt the student's plan. This is a stress test of the young aviator's ability to counter an air threat, regain formation support and integrity, and continue the attack.'

'Mission exercises in the simulated attack profile phase are particularly valuable for a nav student. He assists in the planning process and is an active participant in the flying phase of the mission. As a crew member in the attack formation, he must back up the student pilot's navigation, maintain a good lookout for the bounce, and use the radio to maneuver the formation for defense if the bounce is sighted. Flying with the bounce instructor, a student nav assists in navigating to an intercept point. He must also monitor the actions of the unengaged member in the attack flight during an engagement, keeping the bounce pilot informed so as to prevent an opposing flight member from gaining an advantageous position for simulated air-to-air weapons firing.

'At the end of all these phases a new tactical aviator emerges. The student pilot will now get his final aircraft assignment based on the needs of the RAF and a thorough examination of his tactical skills. Armed with terminology, a bag of tricks, and tactical thinking, he's ready to learn the peculiarities of his new weapon system. While transitioning to his new aircraft, many elements of his TWU training will be rehashed. However, the time he must devote to basic tactical concepts has been significantly reduced.

'Not only is it worth it to the student, it's also worth it to the RAF. Basic tactical training in the Hawk is incredibly

cheap when compared with the cost of conducting such training in any other RAF fighter.

'When my peers and I left basic flying training for fighter assignments, we weren't nearly so well prepared as a TWU graduate. A lot of valuable time in our fighter conversion training was spent learning about basic concepts of weapons, tactics, tactical formations, and low-level flying. Because we didn't know these basics, we weren't able to integrate them adequately into the operating capabilities of our weapon systems. In most cases we could do so only after a few years of flying in our designated weapon system. That's a long time and an expensive process. By comparison, the TWU is pure gold.

'In my mind, I'm convinced the RAF has developed an outstanding program for budding fighter pilots. They have thoroughly impressed me and my associates in the exchange program.

'As long as the RAF continues with such comprehensive TWU training, I've no doubt RAF fighter pilots will continue their world-renowned tradition of excellence in tactical aviation.'

Air Staff Target 412

The Hawk has many years flying ahead of it, both at Chivenor and at Valley, but the basic jet trainer, the Jet Provost, will need replacing by the end of the decade. In October 1983 Air Staff Target 412 was published in outline for an aircraft to fill the role. In mid-1984 it was still not certain whether economic constraints would dictate a deferment of AST 412 with the interim filled by a refurbishment programme for the Provost but several contenders for the AST were already being evaluated at Boscombe Down. The outline target specified a 'Hawk-like' cockpit which was interpreted in the aviation press as implying a tandem, rather than side-by-side seating and a 'desirable but not essential' escape system. It was possible that the lower procurement and operating costs of a turboprop-engined aircraft might influence Service preference in that direction. The aircraft performance requirements are largely dictated by UK weather and density of flying and, as a trainer, it must be able to sustain a high sortie rate while retaining sufficient fuel for a wide diversion radius. In addition it must possess an aerobatic manoeuvrability of $+6/-3g$ and an external stores carrying capability 'would be valuable'. Three aircraft tipped in 1984 by the aviation specialists as primary contenders should a contract be placed were the Swiss Pilatus PC-7, the Embraer EMB-312 Tucano and the British NDN IT Turbo Firecracker. In view of the RAF requirement for 155 basic jet trainers the competition for the order was extremely keen and the Service was fortunate to be able to choose from a handful of high quality contenders.

Operational Training

The excellence admired by the USAF officer quoted is reinforced on the various Operational Conversion Units where the aircrew learn the complexities of their actual combat aircraft, and is sustained through daily training and frequent exercises when they finally reach their front line squadrons. Sometimes those exercises will take place over the UK or Northern Europe, sometimes they will go further afield. The air defence squadrons regularly visit RAF Akrotiri where they take advantage of clear Cyprus skies and the proximity of over-sea ranges for Armament Practice Camps. Even in the age of the Tornado F2, Sidewinder and Sky Flash, the interceptor pilot must still be able to close on an opponent and if necessary despatch him with guns.

Nevada

While Lightnings and Phantoms migrate annually to the Mediterranean for hard flying in conditions perfectly suited for clear air manoeuvre and interception, Jaguars, Buccaneers and Vulcans have, since 1977, been moving in the opposite direction, across the Atlantic to an air base deep in the Nevada desert.

The reason lies in the fact that by 1975 the proportion of combat experienced crews in USAF Tactical Air Command had dropped to 30%. Yet a major lesson learned and relearned in World War 2, Korea and Vietnam had been that aircrew suffered disproportionately high losses in their first 10 combat missions but thereafter their chances of survival were higher. The Commander-in-Chief of Tactical Air Command at the time, General R. J. Dickson, therefore established a novel training complex at Nellis Air Force Base which quite simply would simulate as much as possible of the environment likely to be met by USAF pilots in a future war. Since then, in a total area of nearly 4,000 square miles, a complete 'enemy' territory has been constructed.

The 'Red Flag' training area includes simulated industrial complexes, rail marshalling yards, tracks, tunnels, rolling stock, airfields, armoured divisions, supply bases and columns, command and control posts, radar stations and surface-to-air missile sites. The area is 'protected' by fighters simulating 'aggressor' tactics. The 'Red Flag' exercises therefore cater for many kinds of offensive support, interdiction and air-to-air combat in as near real conditions as could be constructed without actual hostilities.

Left:
RAF Hereford: SNCOs learning leadership for airfield defence.

Above:
WRAF SNCO at RAF Hereford is briefed by syndicate leader on General Service Training Course.

Friendly 'Blue Forces' can expect to be faced with simulated SAM-4, 6 and 7s, 57mm, 75mm and ZSU-23mm radar-laid anti-aircraft weapons and F-5 'Fishbeds', F-106 'Floggers' and plainly hostile F-15s and F-14s depending on whose side is 'winning'.

Nor is the victor decided by the loudest or most fluent voice in the debriefs back at Nellis at the end of the day, but by the analysis of a great deal of electronically gleaned real-time data. For example, air-to-air activity is recorded by the Cubic Corporation's Air Combat Manoeuvring Instrumentation. Video systems at the SAM and AAA sites track the attacking aircraft, recording both duration and range of tracking to determine the surface-to-air kill rate and also assessing the degree of destruction on the surface-to-air defences themselves by the air attacks. Simulation is actually carried through to the launch by the 'SAMs' of small unguided 'Smokey SAMs'; which trail a smoke plume to about 1,000ft. Communication jamming from the ground completes the difficulties in the way of the Blue Forces tasked with one or more of the target complexes in the range.

Since August 1977, RAF squadrons have participated regularly in 'Red Flag' exercises. In 1977, for example, Buccaneers were able to test the effectiveness of their recently installed radar warning receivers and electronic countermeasure pods. Sorties were flown at more than 500kt down to a nominal 100ft above ground level over terrain reminiscent of many a Western movie. Both cluster weapons and 1,000lb bombs were used against life-sized targets from attack runs demanding evasion from SAMs or interceptors. Buccaneer and Vulcan crews alike returned to Europe reassured about the effectiveness of the tactics and left behind a very high regard for their low level skills.

In the following year Jaguars took part and then in November 1978 Vulcans flew night operations on the range for the first time, using terrain-following radar for long periods which also culminated in evasive manoeuvring to counter electronic warfare threats. Unlike in operations over the United Kingdom, where large amounts of tinfoil dropped from a night sky would not be well received, the Vulcans were also able to make full use of their own active ECM equipment. As before, all crews returned to the United Kingdom with increased confidence in their equipment and tactics.

Nor is experience limited to low level combat flying. The RAF squadrons participating in 'Red Flag' do not fly independently, but as part of a composite force which may include other low level attack aircraft, 'Wild Weasel' anti-surface-to-air defence specialists and combat air patrols. Not only must the RAF aircraft co-ordinate their own sorties most closely with the others in the 'wave' – especially at night when flying without navigation lights – but the majority of pilots have at least one chance to plan and lead the entire mission. Not surprisingly, therefore, participation in 'Red Flag' is very highly prized by Royal Air Force squadrons.

Cold Lake
Anyone who has watched a Western movie set in Nevada will realise that although the terrain might present more problems to low flying aircraft than the North German Plain, the weather is generally much kinder. Consequently, RAF participation in 1979 and 1980 in exercises

several hundred miles to the north at Canadian Forces Base Cold Lake in Alberta offered more realistic climatic conditions. Exercise 'Maple Flag' is flown over several thousand square miles of almost uninhabited forest and lakeland where snow, low cloud, rain and other familiar European meteorological conditions are all too frequent. During 1980 the Canadian forces steadily developed the facilities on the ranges. Surface-to-air missiles and vehicle and tank mock-ups were increased and plans were made to install threat simulators and electronic real-time combat analysis. In 1979 RAF Jaguars and in 1980 Harriers participated in 'Maple Flag' for the first time. Although ground threats could not be simulated as at Nellis, the plentiful availability of 'aggressor' interceptors ensured that combat conditions were realistically created.

As Canadian plans are all turned into operational equipment, Cold Lake is becoming an extremely valuable and most realistic training ground for RAF crews. For the Service to capitalise on Tornado GR1's many qualities to the full, it must be flown fast and very low. The opportunity to train on ranges such as Cold Lake not only ensures that the British taxpayer derives the greatest value from his defence spending, but that his sleep is much less disturbed by it. Maximum effectiveness with the minimum of inconvenience may not be the most patriotic of sentiments but in a crowded island with a population quite rightly concerned with the quality of peacetime life as well as with its security, it is an important one.

And, certainly, the more efficient, the more highly trained, the more prepared for war the Royal Air Force is seen to be in the 1980s and 1990s, the less likely it is ever to be called upon to fight.

Training the Ground Crews

In 1984, of a total RAF strength of approximately 93,000, only some 8,500 were aircrew. It is a truism that aircrew, however highly professional, are dependent in the last resort on the quality of the ground crews who prepare the aircraft and the supporting equipment. Happily, such is the attraction of the RAF to young men and women that the Service can and does maintain very high standards for both airman and officer entry. It is not just the demand of high technology which determines the criteria, nor is it the environment which expects every airman to be a tradesman making an individual contribution either directly or indirectly to operational effectiveness, but also the changed circumstances of modern air warfare. Only a decade ago the flight line was still a reality, with aircraft in neat lines on the tarmac available for turn round and minor servicing under the eagle eye of a squadron SNCO. In the mid 1980s an increasing number of RAF airfields appear at first glance to be deserted, as ground crew work quietly away inside the hardened shelters from which the Jaguar, Harrier, Phantom and Tornado is towed for immediate taxi and take-off. More individual responsibility is required with less seniority, and it is gratifying to see airmen and airwomen responding to the challenge. But in addition all ground crews, officers and airmen are expected to play a part in guarding the unit against enemy paratroop or other hostile incursion. A stint in the cookhouse, or the orderly room, or stores can now be followed by a much longer one in a muddy slit trench or on patrol round a perimeter wire. All, including WRAF, are now trained to use firearms and in a shooting war they would be prepared to contribute to the unit's defence, in addition to their primary tasks.

Not surprisingly therefore, RAF ground crew training has been modified to cater for these new circumstances. After passing out from the well known trade training schools at Locking, St Athan, Cosford and Halton, ground tradesmen can expect to face stiff general service and technical supervisory training courses to prepare them for the demands of junior and senior NCO leadership and management. The overall scope of RAF peacetime ground crew training can be summarised numerically: each year about 20,000 servicemen and women pass through 500 different ground training courses preparing them for or advancing them in 19 main trade groups or, if commissioned, for specialist engineering, supply, air traffic control, secretarial, security and training duties.

A junior RAF officer will usually be fully occupied with developing his or her specialist competence and executive ability. With increasing seniority, however, will come the assumption of wider responsibilities which will in turn demand a greater breadth and depth of knowledge about his own Service, the Royal Navy, Army and ultimately our allies. The first step for a flight lieutenant will be the Officers' Command School at RAF Henlow where he will learn about the broader challenges of junior command. Later he will expand his staff skills by completing an individual staff studies course. As a squadron leader he may be selected for the six weeks basic staff course and, ultimately, as a senior squadron leader or wing commander he may be one of the 50 or so officers who are selected each year to attend the Advanced Staff Course at Bracknell, which will prepare him for the highest positions in the Royal Air Force. In 1922, the first Commandant of the Royal Air Force Staff College, Air Cdre Brook Popham observed:

'It is a very true saying that the art of war is the art of dealing with human nature. In a Service like ours where we are constantly dealing with machines, we are apt to forget the human element. In addition a tendency has grown up lately to deal with humanity from the cold scientific standpoint, to try to reduce human nature to an exact science. I agree that this can be done up to a certain point but there is a limit beyond which the factors of individuality, of free will, intervenes and which defies all human calculation.'

Aircraft and equipment can be bought; whether the Royal Air Force meets the challenges of the next seven decades with the same professional effectiveness with which it has faced the last will depend on the quality of the men and women whom it recruits, trains and retains.

Material Resources

During the 1980s the Royal Air Force will complete its greatest re-equipment and expansion programme since the 1950s. The Harrier GR5s, the Tornado GR1s and F2s, the Phantom F-4Js, the Nimrod AEWs, the VC10 tankers, the Tristars, the BAe 146s, will all enter operational service together with their weapons and ground support equipment. Other aircraft will receive regular modifications to extend their operational life until near the end of the century. Meanwhile plans will progress for the next generation of trainer aircraft, fighters and helicopters. On the ground, the reconstruction of the air defence environment will continue, together with the construction of new command and control centres and the progressive 'hardening' of key airfields.

Deterrence permitting, it is possible to envisage a design and development phase of 10 years for any military aircraft followed by perhaps another 25 years' operational service. The implications of this become apparent if one imagines going to the office one day in December 1984 and leaving at teatime having finalised proposals for equipment which must still be fulfilling the RAF's needs in December 2015. Taking a step backwards, the Vulcan force was withdrawn from service in 1984 after being designed in the late 1940s, while the Nimrod – conceived in its earliest shape in the 1940s – looks like outlasting the VC10. Tornado, designed in the 1960s, will still be the backbone of the RAF 30 years later. In the USA, the B-52 can boast a similar lifespan while several Soviet aircraft are entering their third decade of active service, even though many new types have joined them. Not surprisingly, therefore, the supply of equipment for air forces in general and for the Royal Air Force in particular is a very complex and lengthy business. Although the details of the procurement process may vary slightly in detail, the basic procedure is as follows.

First, the RAF staffs will study the likely operational environment in the period in which a weapon system is likely to be entering service. For example, when Tornado was being considered, an assessment was made of the likely European battle arena in the late 1970s. It was considered that a potential aggressor could be expected to have extensive surface-to-air defences but would nevertheless be dependent on his airfields to provide essential air power and on extensive reinforcements to support a large scale armoured offensive which would continue to form the basis of his strategy. Moreover, he could be expected to mount continuous operations by day and night regardless of weather. Obviously, such a broad analysis would be refined by considerable detail from many sources, but from even such a simplified assessment, the genesis of Tornado can be seen. An aircraft was required which had to be able to penetrate heavy air defences in all weathers by day and by night to attack enemy airfields and to interdict his reinforcements. The implications of that requirement, in terms of range, avionics, weapon fits and structural demands, are obviously considerable. Moreover, in Tornado's case, the needs of three countries were to be co-ordinated in the interests of cost-effectiveness per unit.

If the project is a national one, however, then the air staff constructs a 'staff target' (AST) as a basic for further analysis and development. Under the direction of the Procurement Executive of the MoD, the scientific and technical implications of the AST are examined. In an era of rapidly evolving technology, some very accurate assessments must be made. For example, if the aircraft will fly operationally in six years time, what advances in avionics or weapons can be expected in that period? What, in short, is the state of the military aviation art now and how far can

A&AEE

further developments be anticipated? Errors in analysis in one direction will produce an airframe which is obsolescent as it begins its flight trials, while in the other one will be trying to design equipment which will be outstripping available technology and therefore will be either too expensive or too unreliable to put into production. Thus, at the earliest point advice is sought from MoD research establishments about the best options to pursue to achieve the greatest possible effectiveness from the funds likely to be available in the long term costings.

Even the most cursory glance at the Tornado will indicate how extremely difficult such analysis must be. Not, as in the happy days of the Bristol Fighter, an airframe, an engine, guns and a few simple instruments. Requirements for airframe and engines, although much more complex, remain, but now: hydraulics, electrical circuits, computers, automated systems, radars, lasers, electronic warning sensors, in-flight refuelling equipment, optical devices and over and above all that, the actual weapons to be delivered. The translation of the AST into a specific weapon system requirement, then into a development aircraft and, finally, into a Tornado on No 617 Squadron requires specialist skills, many of which are focused on one internationally-renowned base near Salisbury in Wiltshire.

Aeroplane and Armament Experimental Establishment

The Aeroplane and Armament Experimental Establishment (A&AEE) at Boscombe Down has a major responsibility for trials of equipment and sub-systems associated with RAF equipment not just about to enter into service, but in some cases several years after the in-service date. A&AEE has grown from a very small unit known as Experimental Flight, CFS which was set up at the Central Flying School, Upavon in 1914. The Flight had a staff of three: one pilot and two scientists who were serving in the Royal Flying Corps. Its equipment consisted of two BE2s and its terms of reference included the development of methods of dropping bombs, firing guns, taking photographs from aircraft and the development of methods of air-to-ground and air-to-air signalling. It gradually expanded and, as the Testing Squadron RFC, moved to Martlesham Heath in 1917 where it remained until the outbreak of war in September 1939 when it moved to Boscombe Down.

Initial flying of a new aircraft is carried out by the manufacturer: for the Tornado, for example, by British Aerospace at Warton in Lancashire, or for the Nimrod at Woodford in Cheshire, but at a previously agreed point the aircraft is handed over to A&AEE. At Boscombe Down a carefully selected team of Service pilots, drawn from the Army and the Royal Navy as well as from the RAF, will work alongside civilian colleagues from the

Procurement Executive to test every aspect of the performance of the aircraft and its sub-systems. One Division, for example, is responsible for the acceptance trials of navigation/attack and radio/radar installations in new military aircraft and of modification of existing aircraft by new equipments. Assessment of the performance of navigation/attack system is complex, involving parallel activities of flight testing and computer modelling. The Division also evaluates new equipment and systems being considered for installation in future military aircraft, and selected civil navigation systems. For this work it operates a number of highly instrumented laboratory aircraft including a modified Phantom, Comet 4 and Sea King. Another Division is responsible for the evaluation of aircraft armaments which demands mechanical and electrical engineering appraisals of weapons and their associated aircraft installations to establish safety and suitability for Service use. Flight trials are conducted to assess conditions of carriage, normal release and jettison of bombs and fuel tanks and of the carriage and firing of missiles, guns and rockets. Interoperability trials are conducted with weapons of other NATO nations and a wide variety of aircraft is used including Sea Harrier, Phantom, Jaguar, Tornado and Buccaneer. In due course JP233 will pass through equally rigorous trials before acceptance as the major first-generation anti-airfield weapon to be carried by Tornado.

But variable as Wiltshire weather can be, it cannot provide the extremes of temperature that the Harriers of No 1 Squadron or the Jaguars of Nos 6 and 54 Squadrons may have to face if rapidly deployed to an Arctic winter or a Middle Eastern summer. An indispensable facility at Boscombe Down is, therefore, the Environmental Test Centre which can subject an entire aircraft and sub-systems to temperatures ranging from −40°C to +35°C and 100% humidity. And, whether operating in Arctic, European or sub-tropical conditions, aircraft, armament and avionics systems must remain safe and serviceable in varying electro-magnetic conditions. These are tested by installations which can simulate radio frequencies, static discharges and the electro-magnetic pulses similar to those produced by a nuclear explosion.

But there comes a point when simulation has to stop, and the actual handling in the air of the complete aircraft and sub-systems must be assessed. This is the responsibility of the three squadrons of Test Flying and Training Divisions which provide the flying effort in support of these divisions. A Squadron flies fighters, strike and trainer aircraft; B Squadron operates bombers, tankers, maritime and transport aircraft; and D Squadron handles all helicopters irrespective of Service user. B Squadron also provides transport facilities within the United Kingdom and in support of overseas trials which are often mounted away from normal air service routes. In addition to the provision of flying effort in support of the assessment divisions, the test pilots make a unique personal contribution by their assessments which are based on specialised knowledge of the operational environment and of the suitability of aircraft for particular roles.

In 1982 the Boscombe crews made a vital contribution to the Falklands campaign by their rapid flight testing and clearance of several new aircraft/weapon and aircraft/refuelling combinations. In 1983 development flying of Tornado acquired an additional dimension with the arrival of the first air defence variant, F2. Later that year Martin Horseman of *Armed Forces* journal reported on progress which typified Boscombe Down's 'bread and butter' contribution to the RAF's re-equipment programme:

'The latest aircraft to reach Test Flying and Training Division's A Squadron in mid-March was the first prototype, A-01, of the Tornado air defence variant or Tornado F2 as it is designated for RAF service. The A&AEE trials with the aircraft, ZA254, were scheduled to start on 18 March with handling checks before moving on to an assessment of the Tornado F2/Sky Flash AMM combination and then, sometimes later, the acceptance testing of the aircraft with Sidewinder AAMs.

Above left:
A rare opportunity at Boscombe Down: evaluation of the ex-Argentinian Pucara.

Above:
A Hercules closes up on a Tristar prior to its conversion to RAF tanker, simulating AAR trials.
Crown copyright photo by A. Booth

'Ahead of the flight trials the aircraft was undergoing a functional check of signals from the control system to operate the Frazer Nash missile launcher, which during the launch sequence pushes the Sky Flash missile down and clear of its semi-recessed housing built into the aircraft's fuselage underside. ZA254 is fitted with data link for real time monitoring of the trials and has recording systems on board for post-sortie analysis of performance information. The aircraft is being tested up to the limits of manoeuvre and speed; and the aim, according to Wing Commander Ron Burrows, OC A Squadron, is to produce 'carefree handling'. The first stage of the Sky Flash trials with the Tornado F2 is to conduct BNG (ballistic, no guidance) tests throughout the envelope, which extends between Mach 2.2 at altitude down to 800kt at low-level. Of the three Tornado F2 prototypes, A-01 will be the mount for the missile firing trials, and the engine performance tests (the F2 is powered by the up-rated "extended reheat" versions of the RB199 turbofan) while aircraft A-02 and -03 will conduct weapons systems trials; gun trials will follow later though not with A-01.'

Rather more unusual was another flight test programme under way at the same time: of an ex-Argentine Air Force Pucara. After some 25 hours to evaluate its performance characteristics it was decided that it didn't have a great deal of future with the RAF and will probably finish up in a museum alongside other, rather more successful combat aircraft recovered from earlier conflicts.

The Empire Test Pilot School
All the pilots at Boscombe Down have recent appropriate operational backgrounds and most are graduates of one of the most internationally famous of all RAF units: The Empire Test Pilot School (ETPS). This was established at Boscombe Down in 1943 and after one or two deployments has been settled there since 1967. Each year 22 students, of whom some 50% are normally from overseas, attend either the Fixed Wing (FW), Rotary Wing (RW) or Flight Test Engineer (FTE) course. The 300-hour groundschool programme includes aero systems, lectures from military and industrial specialists and visits to aircraft manufacturers and air shows. On average, two hours per day are devoted to the theoretical basis for each of the flying exercises, of which there are approximately 20 for both FW and RW. One of the course aims is for the pilot to understand the language of the scientist and engineer to allow him to discuss problems on an equal footing. He must also learn to be able to identify the aircraft problem areas and limitations, master test flying techniques and to communicate his findings by clear oral and written reports.

His flying experience will be broadened on nine FW or five RW types including a Jaguar, Lightning, Hunter, Andover, Canberra, Hawk, Sea King, Lynx and Gazelle. He will be required to assess handling characteristics such as stability and control assessment, and specific exercises such as manoeuvre boundaries or flight envelope investigation. His performance exercises will include accurate measurement of rates of climb, pressure air corrections and hover performance. The third group of activities, systems, includes autopilots, navigation and attack systems and flight simulators. In addition to the 'straightforward' flying of the aircraft already mentioned the student will handle a specially modified Bassett whose stability and control characteristics can be varied to simulate a wide range of aircraft types and handling qualities by an analogue computer which, connected to the right-hand controls, feeds signals direct to the control surfaces.

During the course, visits are made to leading aircraft, engine and component manufacturers and to Government establishments in the United Kingdom to meet aircraft design teams and test pilots, and to gain experience of the methods used in the various stages of aircraft development. Contacts are also maintained with other test pilot schools, links being particularly strong with the United States Naval Test Pilot School at Patuxent River, Md, and with the *Ecole du Personnel Navigant d'Essais et de Reception* at Istres in Southern France. There is a regular student exchange with both these schools, and staff liaison visits with these – and with the US Air Force Test Pilot School at Edwards AFB, Ca – also take place regularly. In addition, the Empire Test Pilot School exchanges a test flying tutor with the US Naval Test Pilot School.

On graduation from the School, the British pilot will either stay at Boscombe on one of the test squadrons or go to Farnborough or Bedford for other kinds of test and development flying. For example, at the Royal Aircraft Establishment's Flight Systems Department at Bedford a special version of Tornado is being used as a test-bed for advanced cockpit displays, special sensors and a new digital recording system. The aircraft is being flown in a series of trials involving terrain-following techniques, weapon and other external equipment carriage and release, and low altitude air turbulence. In this way RAE can ensure a constant and timely flow of ideas both back into the Service and outside to British Aerospace and avionics companies.

Test Flying the Man
At the other Royal Aircraft Establishment at Farnborough, an additional, equally important test unit is located: the Institute of Aviation Medicine, whose ancestry dates back to the Royal Flying Corps' Physological Laboratory at Hampstead in London in 1918. Today its main task is to provide specialised advice to the Air Staffs on the human factors associated with flying. It conducts research into attitude and breathing systems, behavioural sciences, bio-dynamics, environmental sciences and neurosciences, while a further division is involved in experimental design and systems engineering. A brief survey of the Institute's activities highlights the considerable demands of modern high speed flight on the human body.

The Altitude Division is responsible for a wide variety of projects concerned with the effects of – and protection from – the hazards of exposure to altitude, such as decompression sickness and hypoxia. Fundamental and applied physiological research into the effects of altitude on man is being conducted, and protective oxygen equipment for use by aircrew is being developed and evaluated. The Division has been responsible for such equipment for use in military aircraft such as the Hawk, the Tornado and the Sea Harrier – and in civilian aircraft, such as Concorde. Two of the three sections within the Behavioural Sciences Division of the Institute are the General Psychology and Flight Skills Research Sections staffed by psychologists. Both sections match operational needs with human capabilities and limitations in aviation environments. The main emphasis is to study envisaged tasks, the equipment provided for them, and the work environment – in order to promote safety and efficiency – and to minimize the incidence and consequences of human error. Work encompasses military and civil human-factor problems in the air and on the ground, the latter including air defence and air traffic control. Field investigations, simulations and laboratory experiments are employed, and their results integrated. Because many problems are new, specialist techniques and equipment often have to be devised – and novel research methods pioneered – in order to obtain answers of proven validity. This applies, for example, to the investigation of accidents, to the optimization of aviation maps for cockpit tasks and monitoring, and to the development of codings to denote the trustworthiness of data.

Biodynamics is the study of the biological effect of mechanical forces – in this instance especially those forces associated with aviation. These include impact or 'crash' decelerations, and sustained or centrifugal accelerations. The latter are usually experienced by pilots 'pulling G' as changes in body weight, and can produce disturbances of vision (such as 'grey-out' or 'black-out'),

difficulty in breathing, or loss of consciousness. These prolonged accelerations are studied on the man-carrying centrifuge, in which tests can be carried out under controlled laboratory conditions. Hence, the benefits afforded by different protective measures (such as the 'anti-G' suit, reclined seats or breathing against increased pressure) can be accurately and safely assessed, and the physiological mechanisms responsible for disturbances of function also elucidated.

Accelerations of greater abruptness which may occur in emergencies (for example, ejection or crash) are studied on live subjects or on dummies riding on a sledge which can be stopped in a fraction of a second.

The problems of exposure to extremes of temperature are studied by the Climatic Research Section in two main environmental laboratories: a climatic wind tunnel, and a radiant heat laboratory. Modern high-performance aircraft fly fast and low which, together with heat-producing avionic equipment, can lead to very high cockpit temperatures – even under European winter conditions. The Climatic Research Section is a world leader in the development of specialized equipment for measuring climatic conditions in cockpits and the body temperatures of the pilots. Much of the applied work of the Section is designed to assess the impact of these conditions on the pilot's performance and well-being and, by the development of systems such as water-cooled suits, to improve tolerance. Modern pilots wear many articles of protective clothing which exacerbate heat stress. A prime example is the new assembly for protection against chemical warfare agents, and the assessment of the thermal effects of such clothing assemblies is an important area of the Section's work. At the cold end of the scale, problems arise mainly

Below:
British Aerospace demonstration of ALARM anti-radiation missile mounted on Tornado. *BAe*

Above:
Tornado weapon carrying trials: 12 1,000lb bombs.

in the survival context and the Section is particularly concerned with the pilot who parachutes into the sea. The development and assessment of clothing and equipment for immersion protection is an important task. The UK's commitments in the northern flank of NATO, and recent experiences in the South Atlantic, have meant that the general problems of operating in very cold conditions have become more pressing.

Physiological aspects of the performance of items and assemblies of personal equipment are also investigated at each stage of development. The work of the Neurosciences Division is concerned with those problems of aircrew, or of the aviation environment, which involve vision and the central nervous system. In the field of aircrew workload, the Division is concerned with the maintenance of continuous air operations, and investigations are carried out to identify and evaluate the factors which may impair vigilance of those individuals who have to cope with irregular patterns of work and rest. Work on vision involves both the investigation of visual problems in aircrew and the assessment and development of optical devices, to enhance aircrew performance and to protect them against ocular hazards.

The Maintenance Units
After the completion of acceptance trials, aircraft and associated equipment, as well as the thousands of items of ground stores, are accepted into the RAF via maintenance units in RAF Support Command. Each has a particular specialisation. At No 30 MU Sealand, for example, all airborne radio, radar instruments and other avionics are overhauled, repaired and modified by both civilian and uniformed craftsmen and engineers. Further south at St Athan in South Wales a large number of the RAF's front line aircraft receive their major servicing, including the

Tornado and the Phantom. At RAF Stafford, No 16 MU houses several thousand items of spare parts which can be delivered daily by land or air to any RAF station in UK or West Germany in response to urgent calls from the front line. Overall, RAF Support Command has the capacity to accept, modify, repair, fault diagnose and service almost any item returned in an unserviceable condition from squadrons whenever it is expedient and economical to do so. Intermediate support is provided in Germany by No 431 MU at Bruggen which is responsible in peacetime for the second line – ie not so extensive as 'third line' – servicing of a large proportion of the air and ground equipment used in RAFG. In the event of tension it would deploy its people and kit around the four main airfields. In exactly the same way, large numbers of airmen and airwomen employed on peacetime duties in Support Command would deploy to front line units to provide the extra hands and expertise necessary to raise the intensity of operations to combat readiness for an extended period.

The Sum
During the next decade the front line strength of the RAF will increase by one-sixth; but numerical expansion is but a minor factor in the real growth of British air power manifested by new aircraft, new weapons, new support equipment and a lean structure. The nation has the right to expect the maximum return in security from the resources it allocates to defence. In an uncertain world it remains regrettably certain that military force will continue to be the arbiter in many international disputes: neutrality is not an option for the defenceless, as the plight of many nations in history has testified. British air power, spearheaded by the Royal Air Force, enters the next decade better equipped than at any time since 1945 to give any potential aggressor good reason to pause and to count the probable cost of his temerity. That is the bedrock of deterrence: the continued raison d'etre of the British armed services within the NATO alliance and wherever else in the world British interests may be located.

HELP REPAY THE DEBT WE OWE

OVER 70,000 MEN AND WOMEN OF THE ROYAL AIR FORCE DIED IN THE DEFENCE OF OUR FREEDOM IN WORLD WAR II — MANY THOUSANDS MORE WERE LEFT PHYSICALLY AND MENTALLY DISABLED. THE RAF HAS ALSO INCURRED CASUALTIES IN THE MANY CONFLICTS IN WHICH IT HAS BEEN ENGAGED SINCE 1945 AND IN THE DEMANDING TASK OF MODERN OPERATIONAL FLYING ON WHICH THE PRESERVATION OF PEACE SO MUCH DEPENDS.

The Royal Air Force Benevolent Fund was founded in 1919 to help those who served or are serving in the RAF, their widows and dependants. There are no hard and fast rules about who may be helped or how much help may be given; each person's needs are considered in the light of their particular circumstances, the object being to provide relief in the many cases where assistance from the State is either not forthcoming or is inadequate.

The Fund aims to enable dependants to maintain some semblance of the life to which they have been accustomed, and to help children into careers which their fathers might reasonably have expected them to follow.

The Duke of Kent School, Woolpit, is an independent preparatory boarding school administered by the Fund for the sons and daughters of Royal Air Force personnel of all ranks. Preference for admission is given to children (foundationers) whose fathers died or were seriously disabled whilst serving.

Princess Marina House, Rustington, Sussex, provides convalescence for serving personnel of all ranks of the Royal Air Force, and convalescent and residential accommodation for partially disabled and elderly past members of the Service, their adult dependants and the adult dependants of those still serving. Such residential accommodation is also provided at Alastrean House, Aberdeenshire.

WE NEED YOUR HELP NOW AND WILL CONTINUE TO NEED IT. SO PLEASE REMEMBER THE FUND IN YOUR WILL. ADVICE IS GLADLY GIVEN ON LEGACIES, BEQUESTS AND COVENANTS. DONATIONS ARE OF COURSE WELCOME TOO — EVERYTHING WE RECEIVE MEANS WE HAVE MORE TO GIVE. IF YOU KNOW OF ANYONE WHO MIGHT QUALIFY FOR HELP FROM THE FUND PLEASE LET US KNOW.

Royal Air Force Benevolent Fund

67 Portland Place, London W1N 4AR. Tel: 01-580 8343

— also at —

11 Castle Street, Edinburgh EH2 3AH. Tel: 031-225 6421

Registered under the War Charities Act 1940 and the Charities Act 1960. Registration No. 207327

The effectiveness of British Air Power in the 80's
is dependent on the men and women
who make up the RAF.
To find out more about the Royal Air Force,
call in at any RAF Careers Information Office.